fine
FABRIC

Delicate Materials for Architecture and Interior Design

Imprint

The Deutsche Bibliothek is registering this publication in the Deutsche Nationalbibliographie; detailed bibliographical information can be found on the internet at http://dnb.ddb.de

ISBN 978-3-03768-004-9

© 2009 by Braun Publishing AG
www.braun-publishing.ch

1st edition 2009

Editorial staff:
Sophie Steybe, Marek Heinel
Draft texts by the architects. Text editing: Chris van Uffelen
Translation:
Alice Bayandin
Graphic concept:
Michaela Prinz
Layout:
Natascha Saupe

Chris van Uffelen

fine
FABRIC

Delicate Materials for Architecture and Interior Design

BRAUN

Becoming

Textiles are some of the oldest materials used in architecture. According to Gottfried Semper (1803–1879), the most influential architect and theorist of his time, architecture itself began with textiles. At the time when dwellings consisted of earth mounds and mud walls, the first identifiable walls originated from stretched textiles. In his understanding, stone structures belonged to the substruction; wood elements, as former components of tectonics, were part of the roof; the use of walls as interior dividers, and with it architecture, originated from the upright loom. Semper based his demand that modern walls take on a colorful, textile-like appearance from this postulation.

If today, as then, Semper's assumption and call to polychromy appear a bit daring, his statement that textile production is one of man's oldest technological advances is certainly correct. Present in the Paleolithic era, folding screens were predecessors of weaving looms from the Neolithic period.

Cone-shaped pole structures covered in hides also originated during the New Stone Age, and thereafter tents were found in all cultures. Romans covered tribunes of their amphitheaters with ship sails for sun protection. Medieval emperors travelled across their territories accompanied by tents. For Native Americans living on the prairie, hide-spanned teepees were standard dwellings well into the 16th century, while Mongolian sovereigns resided in luxurious palace-tents. In the second half of the 11th century, large embroidered wall carpets decorated cathedrals and palaces. Artists created panels for tapestry series documenting war campaigns – for example, those made by Jan Cornelisz

Vermeyen for Charles V. Such pieces were considered much more valuable than the paintings which served as their model, including works by Rafael or Rubens.

Textile in wall design was also found outside of figurative representation. The upholsterers' guild was responsible for the creation of all textile and leather cladding for the French court. In China, silk wallpaper was highly valued during the reign of the Han Dynasty and was gradually replaced by paper in the 4th century.

Paper screens, or shoji, have been used in Japan since the 8th century; leather wall hangings arrived in Spain from the Orient with the Moors in the 11th century; textile wall claddings appeared in Italy starting in the 14th century. Paper repeatedly appears on European walls (Melk Abbey, 1425, Christ College in Cambridge, 1505) well before the onset of its history with the import of Chinese products by the East Indian trading companies in the 16th century. In the 17th century, paper with repeating patterns printed on wooden blocks was being produced in Europe, one example being Dominotiers paper.

In 1750, the process of printing on textile was transferred to paper, and in 1799 Nicolas-Louis Robert (1761–1828) patented a machine which produced long strips of print, and which was fundamental to the manufacture of wallpaper which became an indispensible part of the prevailing Biedermeier middle class décor a century later.

Textile and leather wall claddings saw a comeback during the Arts and Crafts and Jugendstil movements, whereas Modernism preferred the aesthetic of bare walls or a monochrome coat of paint (alternatively,

ingrain wallpaper was widely featured in the Bauhaus style). Variously printed wallpaper did not come back in style until Postmodernism.

At this time, even the tent, which persevered as a temporary structure used by traveling circuses and others, experienced a revival – the German pavilion at the Expo 67 in Montreal (Rolf Gutbrod, Fritz Leonhardt, Frei Otto) testified to the renewed interest in tensile architecture. Following this tradition, countless buildings which use synthetic fiber membranes suited for outdoor use continue being built to this day.

In addition to utilization of woven textiles "on" interior spaces, natural-thread fabrics dominate "in" these as well – curtains, flooring, upholstery and table cloths determine the ambience of the enclosed space. The separation between natural textiles (cloth), treated natural materials (paper, leather) and synthetic substances is blurred. These fibrous relatives have been united in this book due to their similarity in composition and application. Speaking generally, fabrics could be defined as fiber composites derived through weaving, knitting, crocheting, organic growth or placement on a common mounting surface. The origin of fibers is also not definitive – they can have animal (wool), plant (hemp), mineral (fiberglass) or synthetic (polyester) origins. Most of these materials and their textile forms share a flowing flexibility and softness, however, even this characteristic is not mandatory – just think of the wallpaper affixed to the wall. Although metal netting does not consist of fibers, it is so alike in its qualities of hanging and flowing, that it is impossible for architects to ignore it as a new form of textile architecture.

Similarly, chain mail worn by knights, its forbearer, is also part of the history of garment. Metal may become a textile by means of its processing, such as when it is woven to serve as a filter in exhaust hoods. On the other hand, many modern textiles are no longer flexible at all – stiff carbon fiber webbing is used to manufacture light bicycle frames, and heavy-duty textiles are used to tape together cracks on façades of historical buildings. By no means did extreme textiles begin shaping these developments only recently. The comfortably movable spacesuits used on Apollo missions at the end of the 1960s consisted of layers of materials such as Mylar, Dacron, Nomex and Teflon, coming together to fulfill the widest range of requirements.

Today, textiles can take on nearly any quality; they can even be transformed into electrical conductors by incorporating circuits.

Standards applied to textiles have risen even in their everyday employ. Modern fabrics must be durable, easy to clean, color fast and as soft as possible. With their smooth surface and low thermal conductivity, reduced even further by surrounding closed-in space, fabrics retain body temperature and are responsible for the interior's warmth and coziness. A wool pillow (heat transfer coefficient = 46) isolates the body of someone sitting on a copper seat (heat transfer co-efficient = 400,000), a material far more efficient in equalizing the temperatures of a mass and its surroundings, be it hot or cold. Sofas and chairs invite us for a leisurely pause, while curtains complete the décor of the room.

Chris van Uffelen

RAINCOAT

Zenith Music Hall, 2008
Address: 1, allée du Zénith, BP 84097 Eckbolsheim, 67034 Strasbourg Cedex 2, France. **Client:** Communi-tée urban de Strasbourg. **Gross floor area:** 14,000 m².
Materials: reinforced concrete, glass/silicone fabric membrane.

Lady in red

ARCHITECTS: Massimiliano & Doriana Fuksas

The design of the Zenith Music Hall is based on a modular, well-balanced concept and is to be understood as a single, unifying and autonomous sculpture. With its playful form and character, the edifice is in line with the great Varieteé theaters, which were built after 1984, when the first Zenith building in Paris was erected. By layering and rotating the ellipsoid metal façade structure the design receives a very dynamic character. This is underlined with the orange translucent textile membrane which covers the steel frame and creates magnificent light effects. Projections on the outer skin convert the façade into a huge billboard communicating upcoming events to passersby. While at daytime the building's appearance emanates a monolithic calmness, at night it mutates to a glowing piece of public architecture.

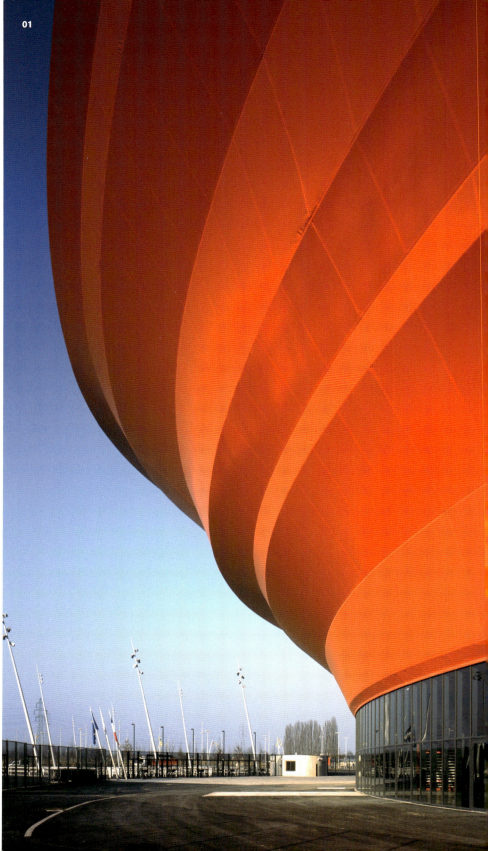

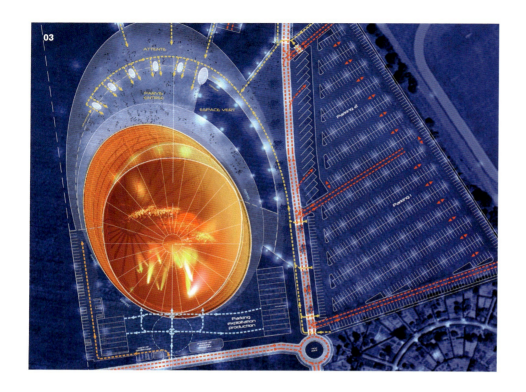

01 Façade with orange membrane skin **02** Membrane structure, internal view **03** Situation plan **04** Detail plans of the façade structure **05** Entrance area **06** External view during night

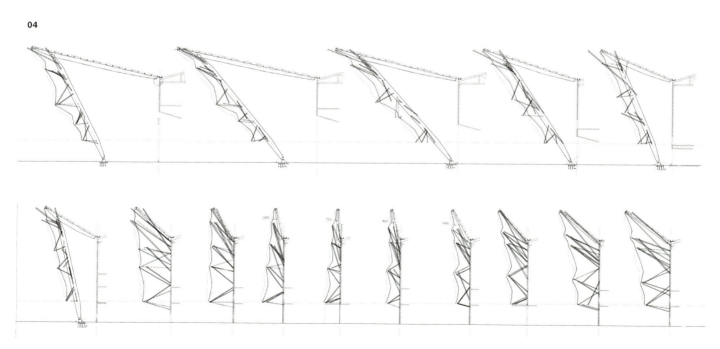

Guy's approaches, 2007
Address: Guy's Hospital, 49 Weston street, SE1 3RB
London, United Kingdom. **Project manager:** Franklin + Andrews. **Structural engineers:** Packman Lucas Consulting Engineers. **Client:** The Guy's and St. Thomas' Hospital NHS Foundation Trust. **Materials:** woven stainless steel braid.

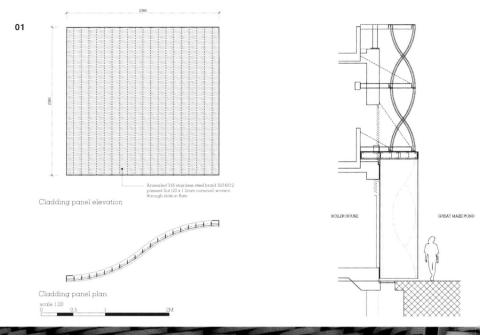

Annealed 316 stainless steel braid 32/16/0.2 pressed flat (20 x 1.5mm nominal) woven through slots in flats

Cladding panel elevation

Cladding panel plan
scale 1:20

0   0.5   1   2M

BOILER HOUSE   GREAT MAZE POND

Machines in the basket
ARCHITECTS: Heatherwick Studio

In the course of restructuring the entrance area of Guy's Hospital, the boiler house was improved. This building is situated in front of the entrance and contains vital machinery. Heatherwick Studio designed the "Boiler Suit" – a tiling system to wrap around the boiler house that provides an adequate shelter for the machinery within, ensures building ventilation and brings the façade to life in a very special way. The tiles used in the façade are human scale, standing 2.4 meters by 2.4 meters. They are gently curved and breathable, formed from stainless steel braid woven through frames. In sunlight this surface becomes animated, reflecting surrounding colors. At night, lighting concealed within the façade provides a dramatic luminous surface, while improving pedestrian safety.

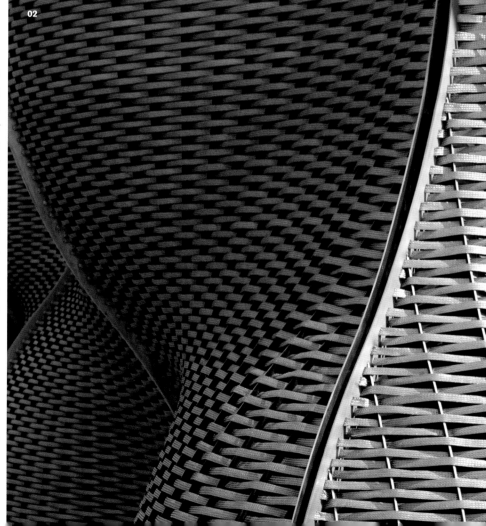

01 Panel structure and section **02** Detail woven tiles **03** "Boiler Suit" by night

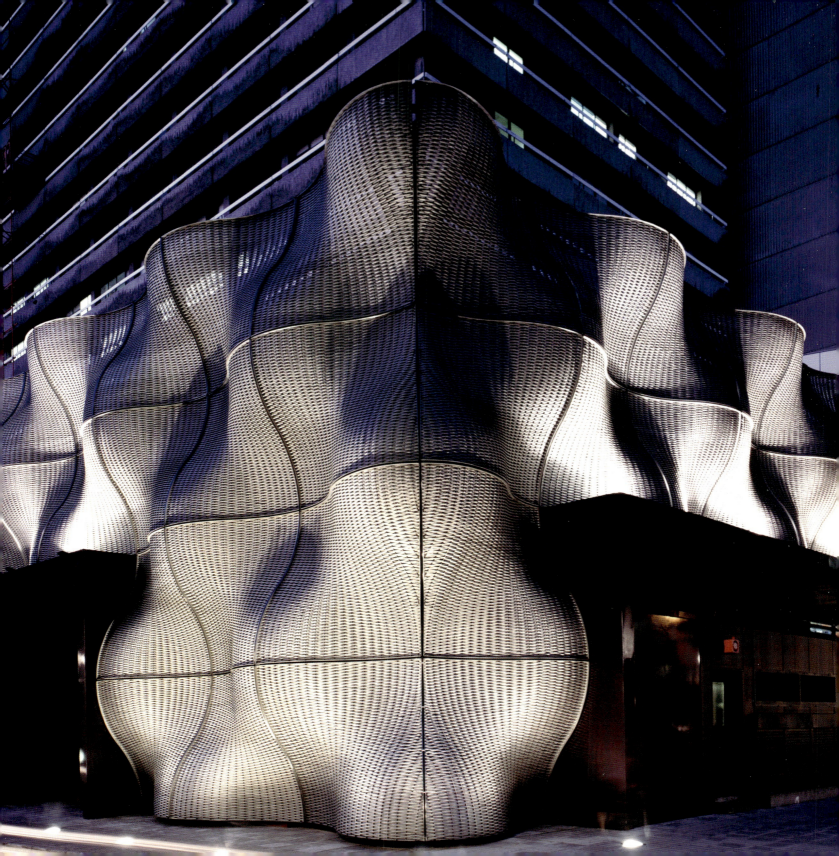

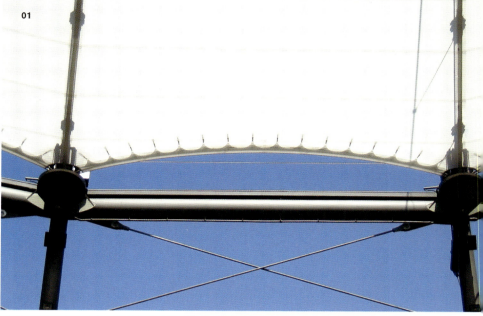

01

Festungsarena Kufstein, 2006
Address: Oberer Stadtplatz 6, 6330 Kufstein, Austria.
Architectural design: Nikolai Kugel. **Structural engineers:** Alfred Rein Ingenieure. **Client:** Stadtwerke Kufstein GmbH. **Gross floor area:** 2,000 m². **Materials:** steel, PTFE-fabric "Tenara" (Gore).

The duke's umbrella

ARCHITECTS: Kugel + Rein, Architekten und Ingenieure

Kufstein fortress is the location of regular open-air events, and it was decided to install a temporarily expandable roof on its site in order to protect the largest possible part of the inner yard from the elements. Strict monument protection regulations were followed. The planners developed a delicate central rope girder with a membrane resembling an oversized umbrella stretched from its center. This structure makes it possible to cover a total area of 2,000 square meters, or the entire inner yard, in 4 minutes' time. When the weather is good, the membrane is pulled back together into the center. Thanks to colorful illumination, the textile roof creates an atmospheric backdrop, underlining the uniqueness of the location.

02

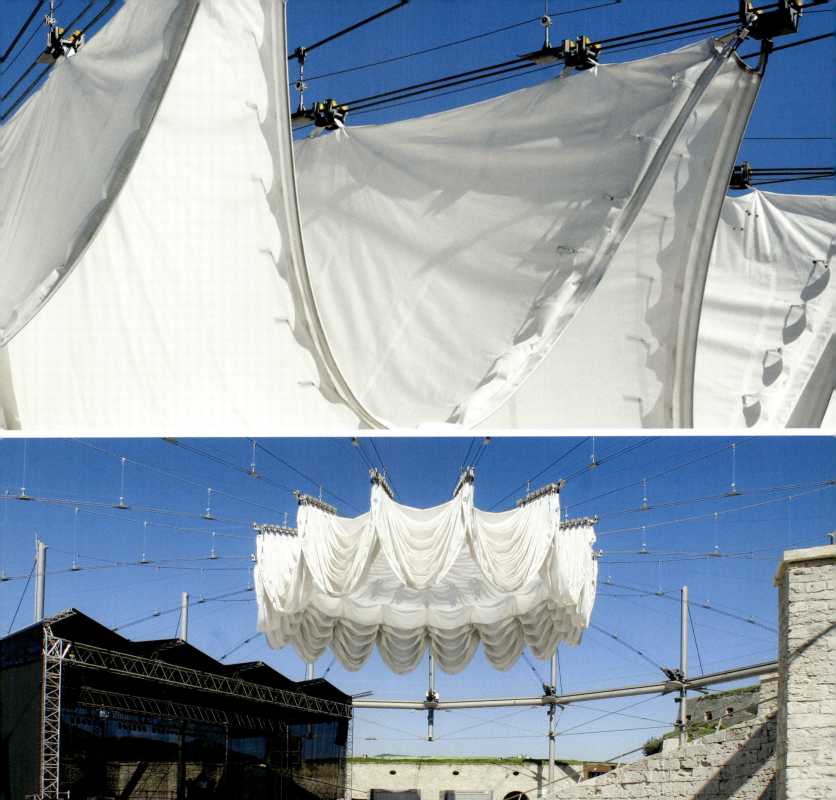

05

06

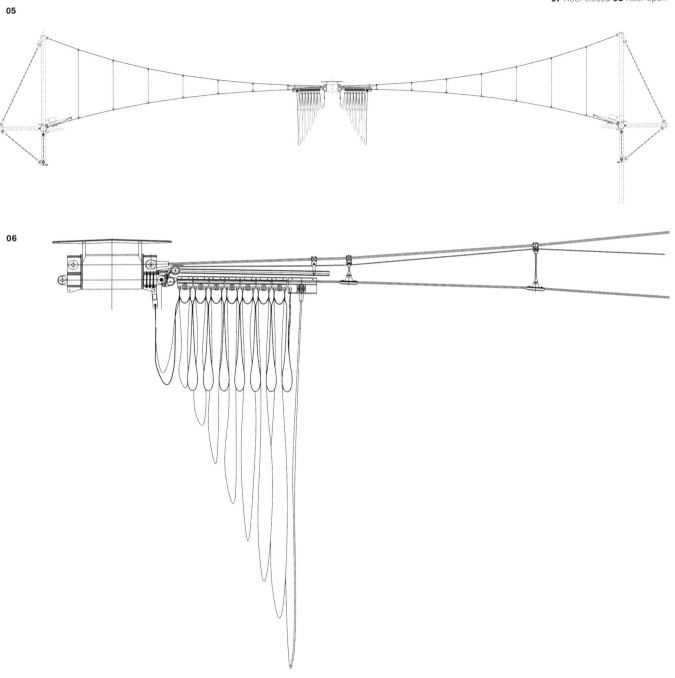

01

Milan meets Mediamesh, 2007
Address: Piazza del Duomo, Milan, Italy. **Manufacturer Mediamesh:** GKD – Gebr. Kufferath AG, ag4 media facade GmbH. **Client:** Urban Screens. **Gross floor area:** 480 m². **Materials:** Mediamesh®.

Stay tuned

ARCHITECTS: ag4 media facade
Ralf Müller

Media façades with integrated LED elements are some of the most colorful and enigmatic developments in the area of textile façades. While other façades sink into grayness at the onset of dusk, these fronts not only bask in light, but are also capable of projecting images or animations. The media façade pictured here consists of Mediamesh, a stainless steel fabric with weaved-in LED profiles capable of coming to life not just in the dark, but also by day. The advantage in comparison to conventional LED boards is the material's transparency and its ability to nestle to the façade, typical for textiles. View from the interior remains unobstructed in spite of the mesh, and the building structure remains clear. The façade's content can be individually programmed via the Internet.

02

05

06

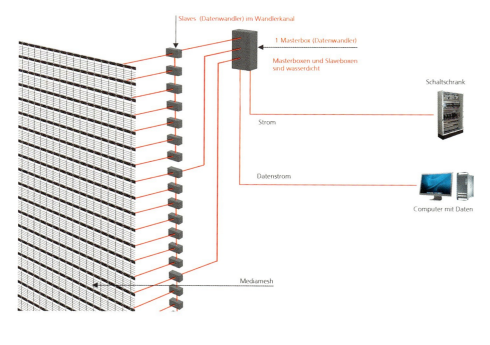

Slaves (Datenwandler) im Wandlerkanal

1 Masterbox (Datenwandler)

Masterboxen und Slaveboxen sind wasserdicht

Schaltschrank

Strom

Datenstrom

Computer mit Daten

Mediamesh

Sydney Olympic Park amenities, 2007
Address: Sydney Olympic Park, Homebush Bay, NSW 2127, Australia. **Client:** Olympic Co-ordination Authority. **Materials:** steel, concrete, translucent fiberglass fabric.

01

Long legs – tight skirt
ARCHITECTS: Durbach Block Architects

The site for these amenities buildings is a vast plane of tarmac, delineated only by parking bays and road markers. Undaunted by the scale of the surrounding buildings and vehicles, the amenities blocks make their presence known as a provocation of form and color, similarly to road worker day-glo vests. With their primary colors and a series of distorting steel portals swelling under a translucent fabric skin, the buildings act as an orientation point for visitors to this vast site. Small urban functions are condensed under their roofs and arcades. By night they invert, as the fabric glows and magnifies their presence, transforming them into taut luminescent islands in eddying flows of spectators. "Flontex", a Teflon-coated fiberglass mat, was used in particular for its transparency and ability to achieve the colorful 'glow' effect.

02

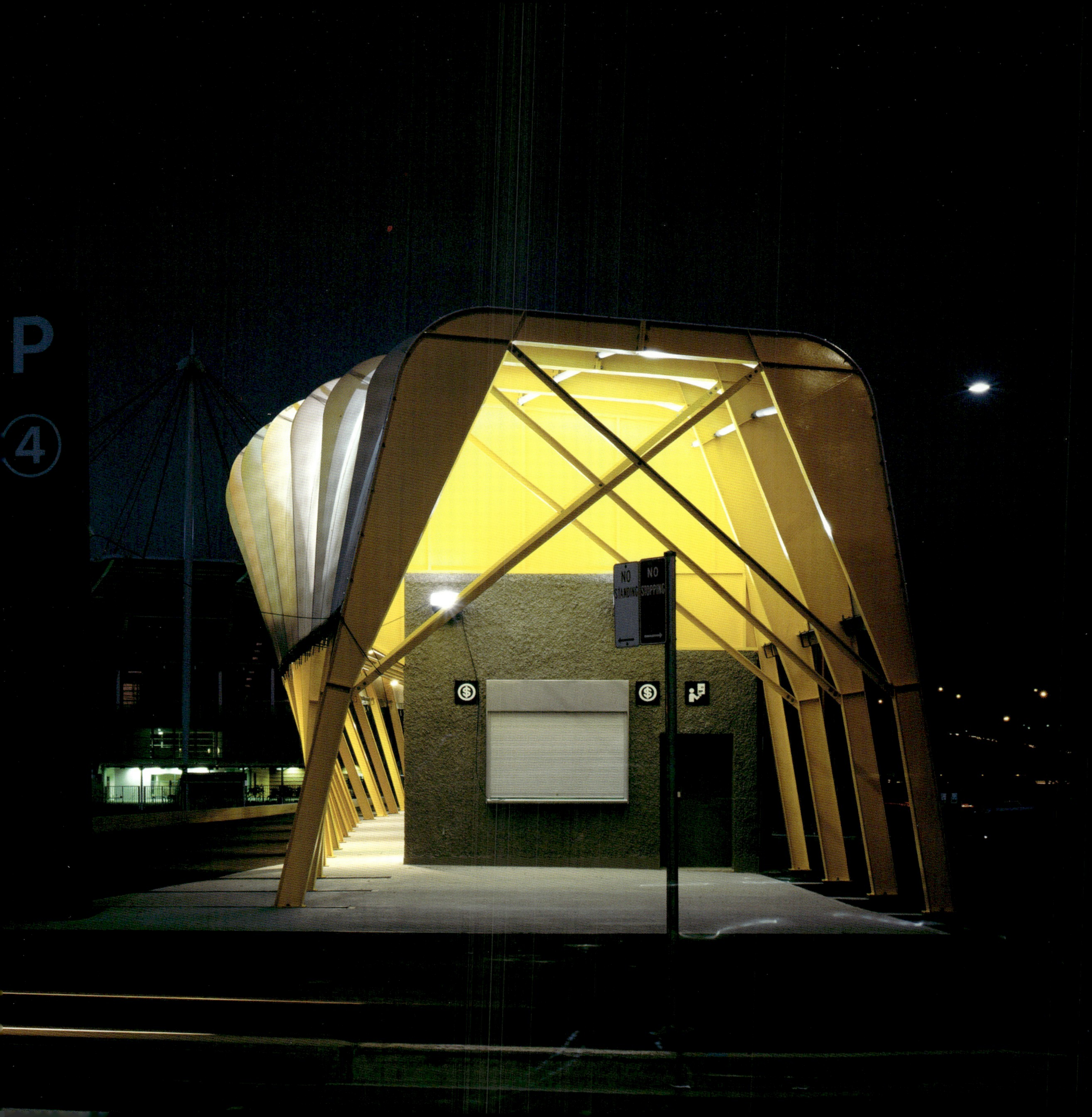
P
4
NO STANDING
NO STOPPING

04

05

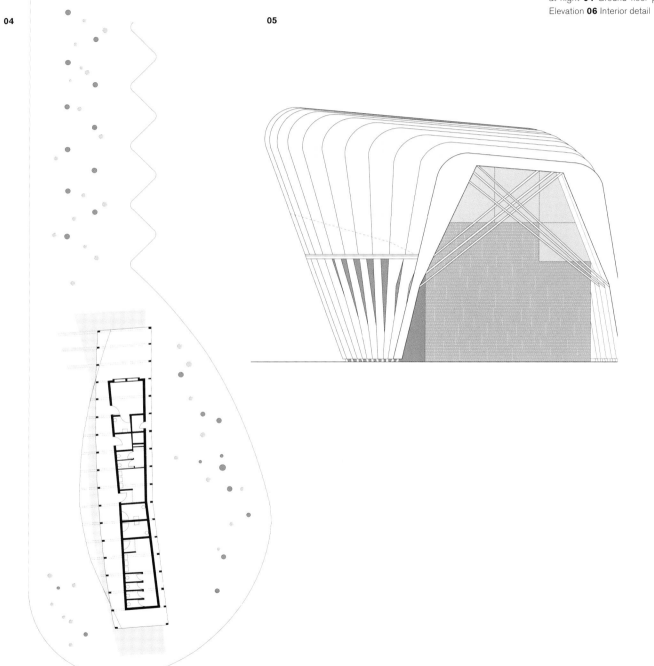

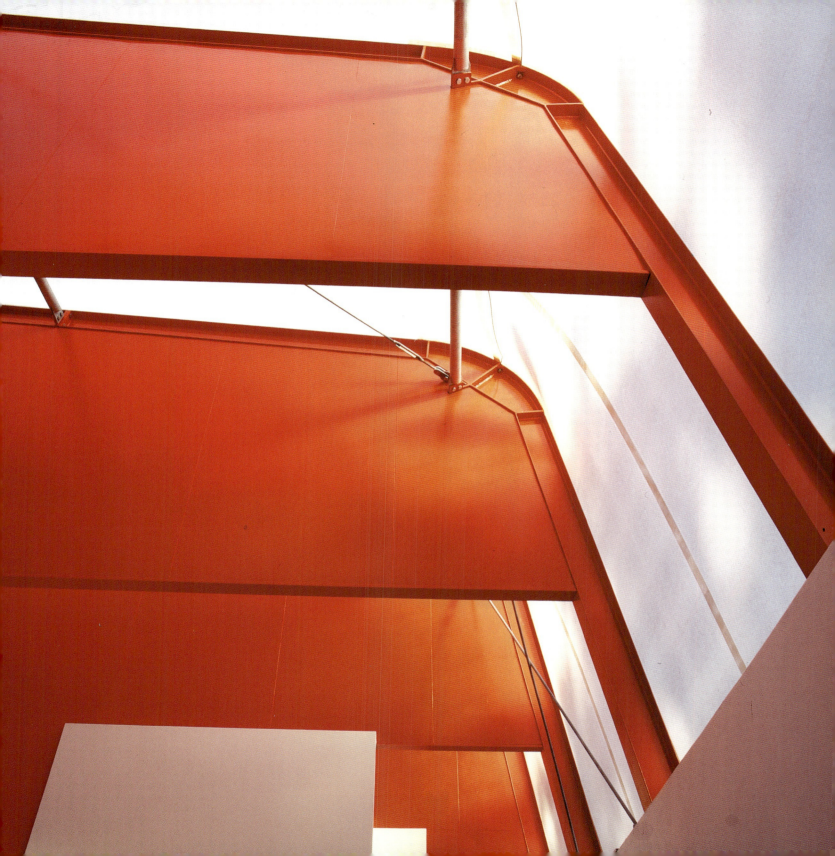

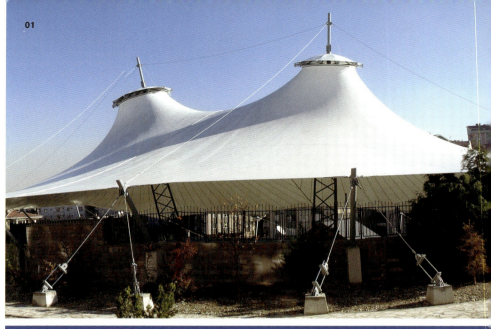

01

Saimekadin amphitheater, 2007
Address: Saimekadin Mah, Asımgündüz Cad, Mamak, Ankara, Turkey. **Client:** City of Ankara. **Gross floor area:** 3,200 m². **Materials:** Ferrari 1202 S Precontraint, Ferrari 1302 S Precontraint.

Some tension in the air

ARCHITECTS: ONART YAPI
Rana Dirin, Prof. Ramon Sastre, Mufit Eribol

The fabric roof covers an amphitheater with a 3000-person capacity and is supported by two 25-meter high truss masts. The conceptual design is directly related to the topographic specifications of the location. The membrane is tensioned by 18 jointed masts at the perimeter. Five of the peripheral masts had to be positioned in front of a building to provide sufficient strength. The masts are connected to the membrane above the roof of the building by steel cables with a 32-millimeter diameter. The two symmetrical sides of the membrane are connected to each other by steel plates. The top section of the membrane uses Ferrari 1302 S, while the rest utilizes Ferrari 1202 S. Approximately four kilometers of high frequency welding joins a total of 324 patterns. The monolithic fabric form was erected in one fell swoop.

02

04

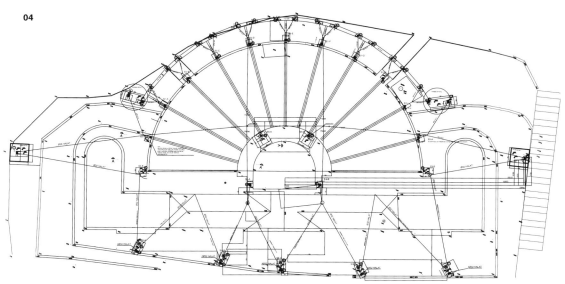

05

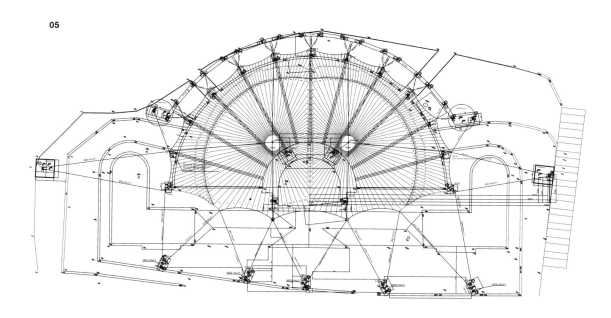

**PH-Z2 [PapierHaus-Zukunftsweisend2], 2009
Client:** Entwicklungsgesellschaft Zollverein. **Gross
floor area:** 256 m². **Materials:** used paper.

Yesterday's newspaper

ARCHITECTS: ASU Planungsbüro,
Dratz Construction

The basic principle of using recycled paper as a building
material is the combination of the material's aesthetics
with its ecological potential. Paper creates a patchwork
of various structures and colors, and the material proves
to be a genuine alternative to conventional substrates.
Its compressive strength is over 50 tons. Heat insula-
tion properties achieve the passive house standard, and
the material can reach a service life of 50 years with
the help of various impregnations protecting against
moisture. The material offers circa 65 percent savings
in comparison to conventional construction methods.
The modular system allows realization of various building geometries. In addition, the material is 100 percent
recyclable.

01 Entrance area 02 Detail inside
03 Perspective inside 04 Circulation diagram 05 Ground floor plan
06 Section 07 Perspective

04

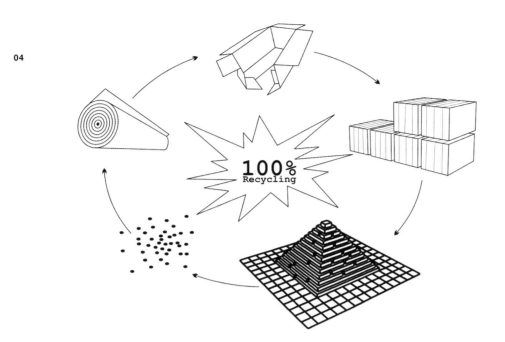

100%
Recycling

05

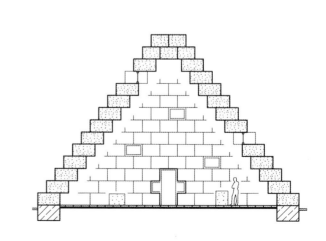

Ausgang

Showroom

140 m²

Sitzblöcke   Tresen

Eingang

06

34

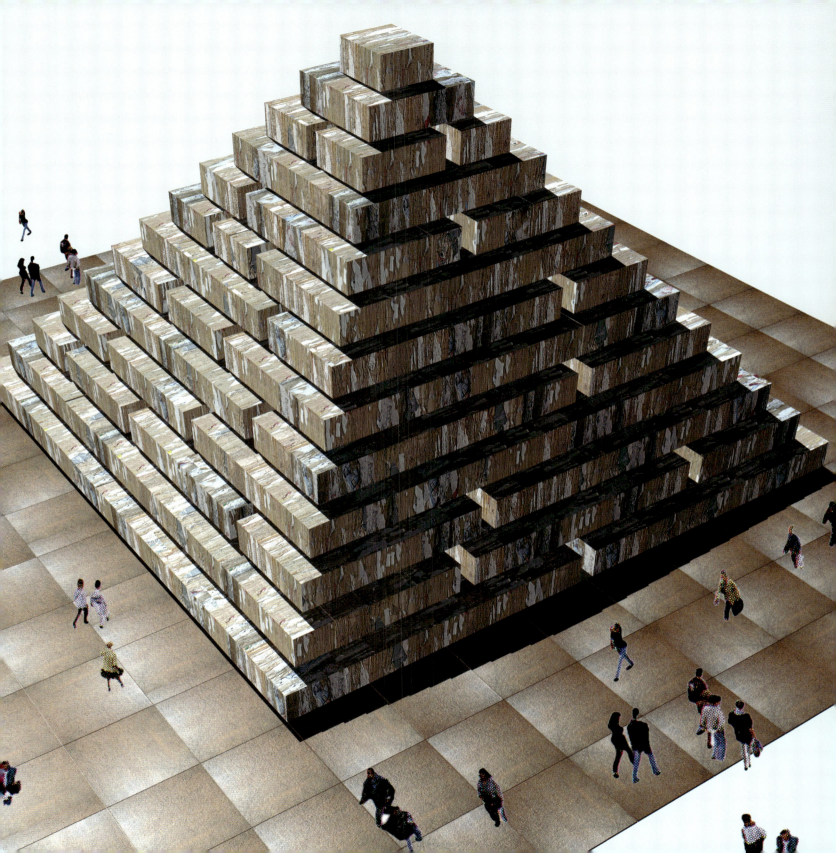

Pink Project – Make It Right, 2007
Address: Lower Ninth Ward, New Orleans, LA 70117, USA. **Client:** Make It Right. **Materials:** Earthtex® fabric.

After the tempest
ARCHITECTS: GRAFT
DESIGNER: Brad Pitt

The Lower Ninth Ward, a rich cultural community long known for its high proportion of resident ownership, was left devastated and homeless in the wake of Hurricane Katrina. To date, initiatives to rebuild this once vibrant area have unfortunately fallen short. As the inaugural event for Brad Pitt's Make It Right Initiative, the Pink Project is a hybrid of art, architecture, cinema, media and fundraising strategies, and acts as an informational commemorative communication tool. Over time and through monetary donations the pink placeholders become reassembled, registering the effects of a collective consciousness in real time, ultimately enabling the construction of 150 real homes. The material used for the tents is Earthtex fabric, a technical nutrient that is PVC-free and 100% recyclable.

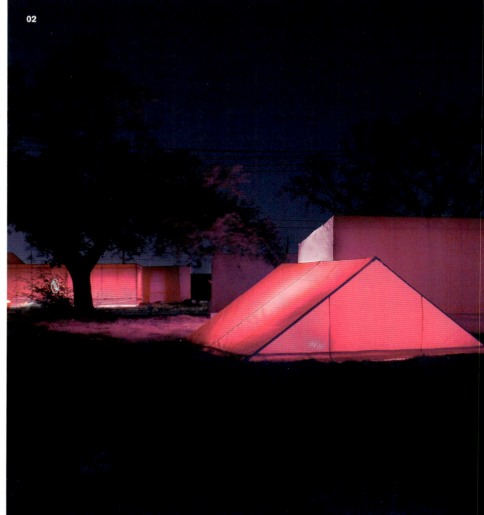

04

05

Serre des jardins à Chaumant-sur-Loire, ongoing
Address: Chaumont-sur-Loire, France. **Other creative:**
Duncan Lewis. **Client:** Festival de Jardins à Chaumant-
sur-Loire. **Gross floor area:** 150 m². **Materials:** bamboo,
PVC-fabric, nenuphars.

Plantihose

ARCHITECTS: Edouard François

Created in the context of a prominent international
garden festival, this greenhouse takes "anti-design"
and "low-tech" as the basis of its attempt to celebrate
the architecture of the ordinary by experimenting with
a whole range of materials and techniques. The ultra-
light structure weighs only one ton and covers an area
of 150 square meters. Bamboo pilers carrying the PVC
cover are interconnected by practically invisible twine.
Eyelets reinforced with rubber gaskets accommodate
guy-wires which anchor the structure externally. Air en-
ters the greenhouse via 30 ventilators embedded in the
cover. The bamboo structure is echoed by the vegeta-
tion carpeting the greenhouse's surroundings and this
continuity fosters the fusion of the exterior and interior.

04

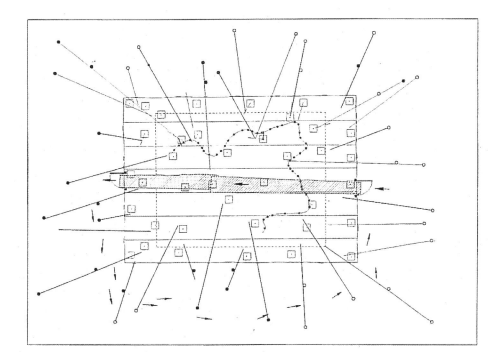

05

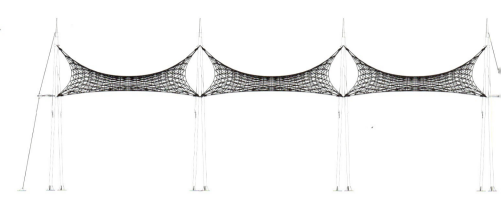

Hip-Notics Cable Ski Park shade, 2008
Address: Cakis Köyü, Manavgat, Antalya, Turkey.
Client: Sun Turizm ve Su Sporlari Tic. A.S. **Gross floor area:** 90 m². **Materials:** Ferrari Precontraint 902 S.

A shade more

ARCHITECTS: ONART YAPI
Rana Dirin, Prof. Ramon Sastre, Mufit Eribol

This sun shade system installed at Hip-Notics Cable Ski Park in Antalya is organized into different elements. Thanks to its high modularity and practicability, the shade can be easily expanded to cover any area by adding further elements. The curved nature of the steel structure is in harmony with the free form of the membrane resulting in a very light, vivid and delicate appearance. All structural components are jointed within the system.

01 Plan **02** Detail **03** General elevation

Aqua-scape, 2006
Address: Tokamachi-city, Niigata prefecture, Japan.
Client: Echigo-Tsumari Art Triennial 2006 Executive
Committee. **Gross floor area:** 10.61 m². **Materials:**
structural polyethylene straw-fiber.

Cocoon on the water

ARCHITECTS: Fujiki Studio, KOU::ARC
Ryumei Fujiki

This prototype of an extraordinary amorphous architecture floats on water and can be viewed as a visionary approach to developing a soft, light and movable structure
which stands in contrast to existing heavy and inflexible
forms. This "boneless" structure was inspired by traditional Japanese Origami and the possibilities opened
by new materials. It consists of polyethylene straw-fiber
woven into a fabric allowing simultaneously structural
strength and flexibility. Aqua-scape was presented in its
final form at the Echigo-Tsumari Art Triennial in 2006
after three years of research and testing, and was dedicated to the children of this region who were victims of
heavy earthquakes and snowfalls in 2004.

01 Night view of the prototype **02** Children exploring the interior **03** Exterior view **04** Section **05** Plan **06** Detail of polyethylene straw-fiber

04

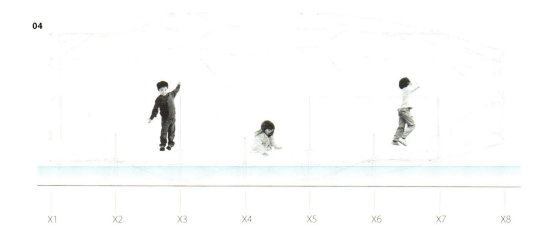

X1　　X2　　X3　　X4　　X5　　X6　　X7　　X8

05

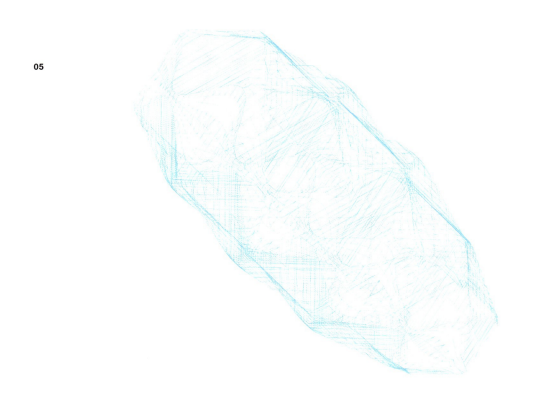

D Line Hanover, 2000
Address: Kattenbrookstrift 33, Hanover, Germany.
Structural engineers: ARUP Düsseldorf, Burmester
und Sellmann Garbsen. **Fabric manufacturer:** GKD -
Gebrüder Kufferath AG, Düren. **Light planning:**
Fahlke & Dettmer Licht in der Architektur. **Client:**
Uestra Hanover / LBS. **Gross floor area:** 420 m² plat-
form. **Materials:** steel, wood, metal mesh.

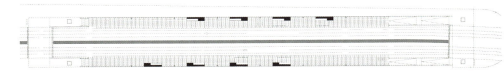

URBAN PUNCTIONS

Urban knights

ARCHITECTS: Despang Architekten

In the course of the preparations for the Expo 2000, the
city of Hanover held a competition for the design of the
southern metro line which would act as an extension
to cope with the influx of visitors. The result was the
D Line – a transportation artery between the city center and the Expo terrain. Twelve metro stations, equal
in size and shape, but differing in the use of materials
and textures came into being, giving the line a touch of
individuality within the uniformity of the transportation
system. The sample station block shown here displays
a special type of fabric skin – a metal mesh structure.
Like most other fabrics, it is semitransparent and thus
provides the interior for the building skeleton, letting the
whole structure appear lighter.

01 Plans **02** Front elevation **03** Perspective **04** Detail

The Pine School, 2007
Address: 12350 SE Federal Highway, Hobe Sound, FL
33455, USA. **Planning partner:** John Umbanhowar.
Client: The Pine School. **Gross floor area:** 9,011 m².
Materials: stucco, fritted structural glazing, perforated aluminum, polished concrete, fiber cement panels, tensile fabric shading components.

01

To aerate a pupil

ARCHITECTS: Scott Hughes_Architects

Southern Florida's mild climate is particularly suited for leveraging the advantages and unique characteristics of tensile structures. The Pine School's mast-supported structures organize the fabric to hover just above the building's façade. This solution shelters the students as they travel from classroom to classroom in a non-air-conditioned environment while providing protection from the region's intense sun and driving rains. The campus design is a functional and formal response to a specific educational vision and program of both active and continuous expansion and inward change. Its structure promotes education and profoundly engages the specifics of its location: "touched" environment redefining itself through the introduction of children and teachers.

02

04

NATURAL LIGHT

SEATING

BREEZES

COMMUNITY GATHERING IN POP COURTYARDS

05

06

Hip-Notics Cable Ski Park conoid, 2008
Address: Cakis Köyü, Manavgat, Antalya, Turkey.
Client: Sun Turizm ve Su Sporlari Tic. A.S. **Gross floor area:** 530 m². **Materials:** Ferrari Precontraint 902 S.

Snappy hat

ARCHITECTS: ONART YAPI

Rana Dirin, Prof. Ramon Sastre, Mufit Eribol

The conoid, a delicate cover protecting the café at the Hip-Notics Cable Ski Park from the elements, has been designed by combining four separate hyperbolic paraboloid textile forms strung above the café's out-door area. Open sections between the forms increase air circulation and give the construction its delicateness. The structure consists of eight columns, four of which are built-in frame columns and four others joint the tension of the textile elements. Combining functional and aesthetic values, the conoid acts as both a cover and a decorative element for the café.

01 Plan **02** Elevation **03** Worm's-eye view **04** Apex point

PS1 MOMA BEATFUSE!, 2006
Address: 22–25 Jackson Ave at the intersection of 46th Ave Long Island City, New York City, NY 11101, USA. **Client:** Museum of Modern Art + PS1 Contemporary Art Center. **Gross floor area:** 1,700 m². **Materials:** polypropylene mesh netting.

Museum of modern mesh
ARCHITECTS: OBRA Architects

BEATFUSE! is covered with a skin of polypropylene mesh scales. They allow wind and rain to move through them without excessively taxing the structure with lateral or lifting loads while providing soft penumbral shade. The inexpensive material is rigid enough to return to its original position after the wind dies down, yet flexible enough to seamlessly adjust to the curved surfaces of the concertina while overlapping in ways that generate gently nuanced patterns of moiré texture. Through testing and sampling, the project team chose an extruded netting product which elicited similar effects of shadow and moiré as early schematic study models. A simple industrial product of plastic mesh is transformed into a dazzling interiorized canopy via simple connections and repeated forms.

04

06

05

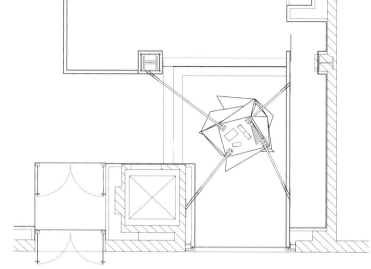

Madison Avenue (Doll)House, 2008
Address: 654 Madison Avenue, New York City, USA.
Structure: Magnusson Klemencic Assoc. **Fabrication:**
Situ Studio. **Design team:** Óskar Arnórsson, Robert
Beach, Jeff Franklin, Basar Girit, Sunnie Joh, Joshua
Prince-Ramus, Jacob Reidel, Wes Rozen, Lavina Sadh-
wani, Alejandro Schieda, Ben Strear, Jay Taylor, James
White, Eugenia Zimmermann. **Client:** Calvin Klein Inc.
Materials: steel, acrylic sheet, four-way stretch nylon.

House couture

ARCHITECTS: REX Architecture P.C.

The Madison Avenue (Doll)House was envisioned as a
concept house that was realized in miniature and show-
cases pieces from Calvin Klein's apparel, accessory, and
home lines. To balance the conflicting desires for views
into the dollhouse versus privacy and solar shading for
the hypothetical occupants, REX wrapped the structure
in a cocoon of white textile. A four-way stretch nylon
fabric was used for its translucence and ability to shift
from taut planes to soft curves as the side panels are
opened and closed. Using both digital models and traditional clothing pattern techniques, fabric consultant
Sunnie Joh cut the skin and dressed the steel frame
without seams.

01 Plan **02** In the showroom **03** Front elevation

Stockton Arena, 2005
Address: 248 W. Freemont, St. Stockton, CA 95203, USA. **Planning partners:** Magnusson Klemencic Associates. **Membrane fabricator:** Eventscape Inc. **Client:** City of Stockton. **Gross floor area:** 22,947 m². **Materials:** aluminum frames, coated woven fiberglass fabric.

Shine a light
ARCHITECTS: 360 Architecture

The design criteria for this new 23,000-square meter arena included the creation of an iconic visual connection between the interior and the surrounding parks incorporating the community's nautical heritage. Sloping custom tensile fabric panels conceal the underside of the arena's seating bowl and provide a 2,200 square meter light wall. This custom light wall projects at a cant toward the ceiling and appears to extend through the roof like the prow of a ship. When lit, the fabric surface and the prow of the roof dissolve the glass curtain wall and connect the interior and exterior spaces in a way that's unusual for this class of building. Furthermore, the lighting of the arena serves as an extraordinary visual beacon, visible from miles away.

04

01 Concourse at daytime **02** Concourse with stairway at night **03** Fiberglass membrane at concourse **04** Ground floor plan **05** Section **06** View towards fiberglass membrane **07** View across the channel

05

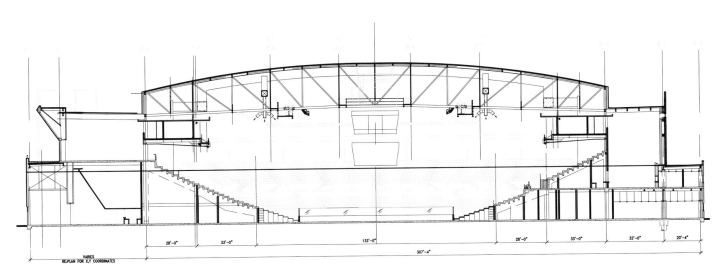

VARIES
RE:PLAN FOR X,Y COORDINATES

28'-0"   33'-0"   133'-0"   28'-0"   33'-0"   32'-0"   20'-4"

307'-4"

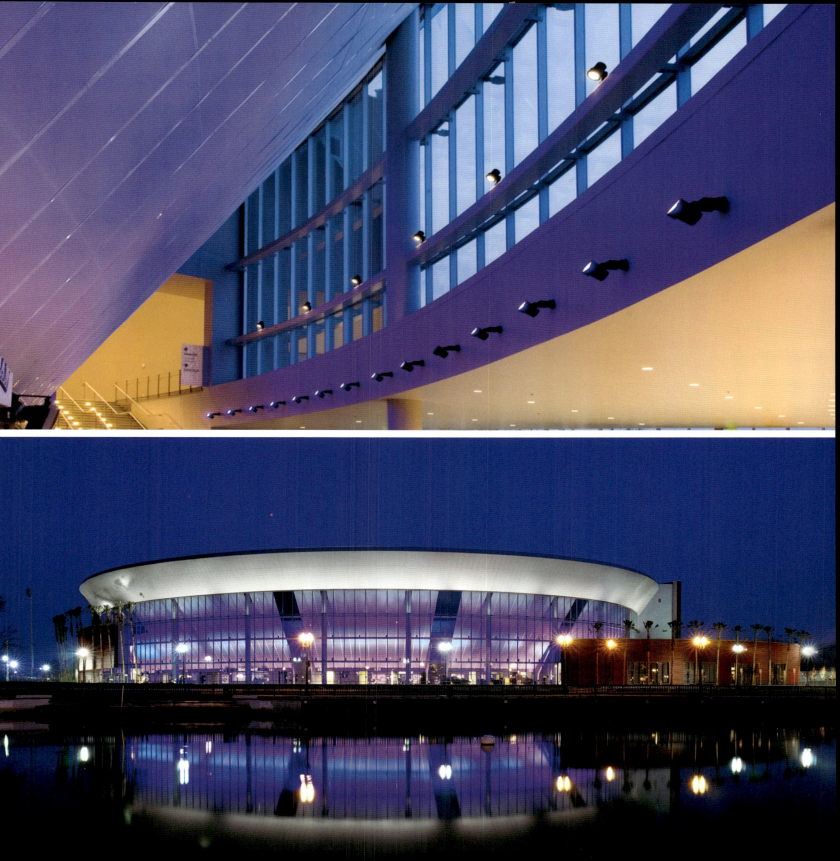

Haus Berkhan, 2006
Address: Schreinergasse 3, 72415 Grosselfingen, Germany. **Planning partner:** Julia Berkhan. **Client:** Julia Berkhan. **Gross floor area:** 156 m². **Materials:** woven fabric (tennis screen).

Blowing in the wind
ARCHITECTS: Markus Fischer

An oversize curtain is attached to the front edge of a 1.5-to-2-meter wide roof overhang on the southeast and southwest façade. Spanning both stories of the building, it serves primarily as sun protection. When closed, it creates a protected outside space, an interstitial zone which mediates the passage from the interior to the outside. Moving of the curtain rails reveals vast possibilities for designing space not just on the outside, but also on the building's interior. Depending on the weather conditions and time of day, various moods can be created using light and temperature. The cubature of the building can be changed to the core; oncoming wind enlivens the building. The semi-transparent material affords breathtaking views.

01 Curtain, west view **02** Curtain, closed **03** Curtain, open **04** Ground floor plan **05** First floor plan **06** Elevations **07 + 08** Patio

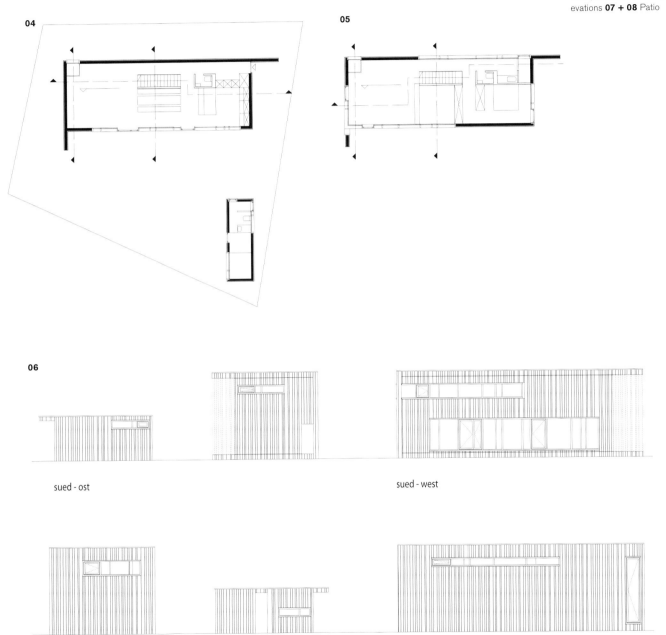

04

05

06

sued - ost

sued - west

nord - west

nord - ost

pPod Mobile Theatre, 2005
Address: anywhere. **Structural engineers:** Buro Happold, Florian Förster. **Client:** Horse & Bamboo Theatre. **Gross floor area:** 24 m². **Materials:** Ferrari Soltis 86, polyester, polyvinyl chloride (PVC, "vinyl").

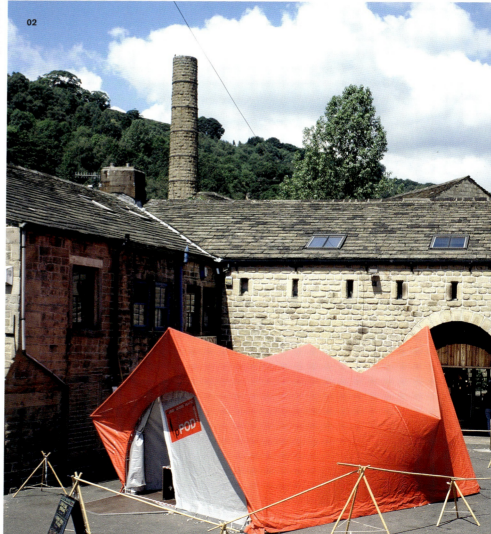

The stage is a small world
ARCHITECTS: magma architecture
Ostermann & Kleinheinz

With the pPod, a mobile stage, the tradition of traveling theaters is brought into the modern age. The geometry of the pPod consists of a series of rectangular frames, which are twisted around an imaginary axis, resulting in a distortion of the sidewalls into double curved planes. The twisted frames are enveloped by the outer fabric, which outlines the hyperbolic parabolic shapes and stretched over the frames to provide weather protection and lateral stability in the longitudinal direction. The outer fabric is perforated with microscopic holes which allow glimpses of the inner form and the structure while preventing the intrusion of water, which is achieved by calculating the hole size in relation to the surface tension of rain drops. The inner structure is opaque and ensures dimmed light conditions for the stage.

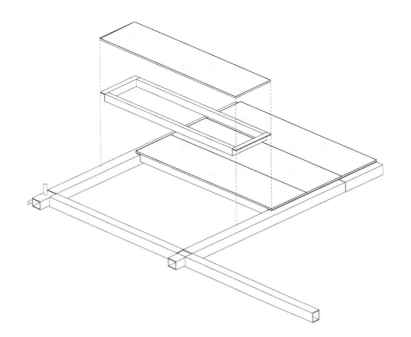

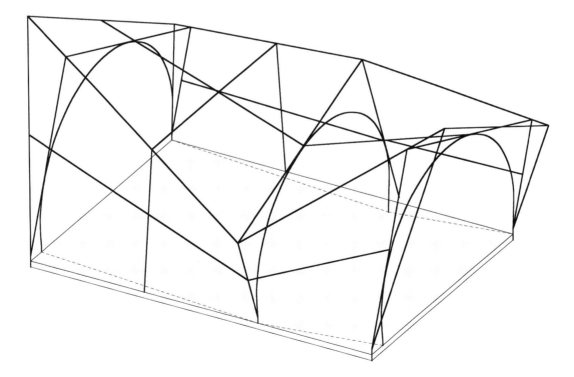

Federal Professional College boarding school for the hotel and catering industry, 2003
Address: Herdstraße 4, 78045 Villingen, Germany.
Client: District of Schwarzwald-Baar. **Gross floor area:** 4,195 m². **Materials:** concrete, fiber cement, glass, plaster, textile sun screen inside and outside.

Color blinds

ARCHITECTS: Melder und Binkert Architekten

Special attention was paid to creating a home-like atmosphere during the construction of the boarding school. Color choice is of particular significance in this matter. On the side facing the inner yard, glazed floors are captured in carefully accented color sequences. The color rhythm created in this way determines the appearance of the rear façade. As if on a stage, the power of orange and blue-green tones diminishes as daylight turns to artificial light. Toward the street, the theme of rhythmic color organization with a 3D effect repeats. Here, textiles bring the infusion of color in the form of sliding screens placed behind the story-high glass doors at clear intervals from each other. The result is a delicately balanced color interplay with a baffling spatial effect.

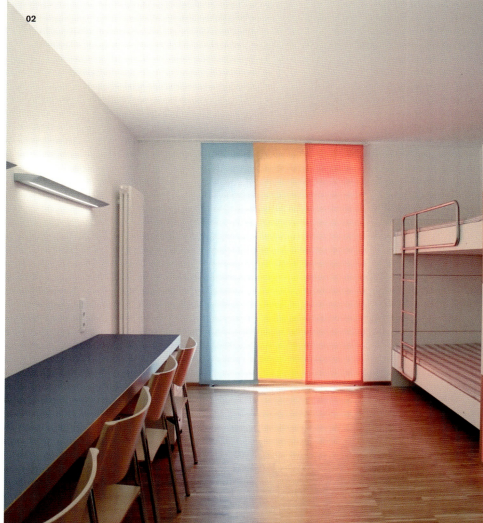

04

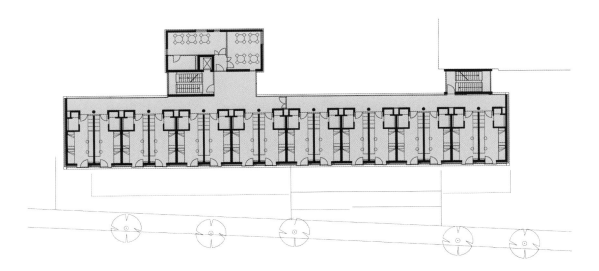

05

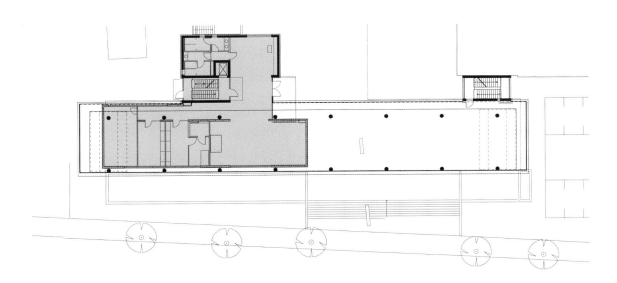

Art depot, 2008
Address: Carl Zeiss Straße 8, 63322 Rödermark Oberroden, Germany. **Planning partners:** Gruppe Bau Dornbirn GBD. **Artists:** Jochen Brennecke, Daniela Finke, B. Felician Siebrecht, Patrick Tschudi, Ernst Hartig (EHa). **Client:** Videor E. Hartig GmbH. **Materials:** reinforched concrete, steel, wood, glass, printed fabric made of polyvinyl chloride (PVC, "vinyl").

Artvertising

ARCHITECTS: Joachim Schwarzenberg Architekten

This art depot has been developed for a company dedicated to promoting the arts. The commitment to digital arts reflects the self-image of the company active in an industry where visions can instantly determine real perceptions of our daily lives. The effect of lightness and fleeting immateriality is primarily connected to the textile façade enveloping the building, which provides needed sun protection while shielding the wooden front beneath it. The textile façade is printed with large-scale art images, transforming the building into a screen and an advertising board for art. Exchanging this "art curtain" at regular intervals is part of the building's concept.

01

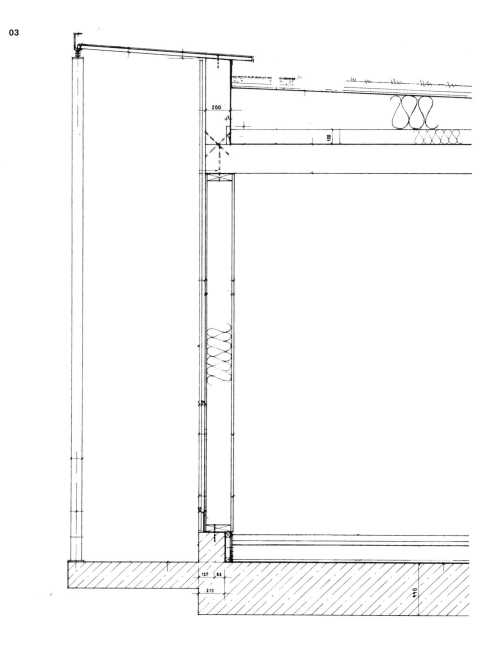

Apartments on the coast, 2005
Address: Livade 15, Izola 6310, Slovenia. **Other creatives:** Rok Oman, Spela Videcnik. **Client:** Slovenian Housing Fund. **Gross floor area:** 5,452 m². **Materials:** concrete construction grid with brick fillings, plaster, precast laminates, robust fabrics for sunshades.

Com(b)fortable

ARCHITECTS: OFIS arhitekti

The apartment blocks are set on a hill overlooking on the one side the Izola Bay, and on the other – surrounding hills. The project proposed a veranda for each apartment, thus providing an outdoor space that is intimate, partially connected with the interior, shaded and naturally ventilated. A textile shade protects the balcony and apartment from prying eyes, while its semi-transparency nevertheless allows the owner to enjoy views of the bay. Perforated side-panels let in summer breeze to ventilate the space. The strong colors create various atmospheres within the apartments. Boxes at the side of each balcony house air-conditioning units. Rooms appear larger due to the perspective effect created by the textile shade, which connects the exterior with the interior.

01 View from balcony with green sunshade **02** Front façade **03** Different elevations of the façade **04** Situation plan **05** Balconies with colorful textile sunshades

03

04

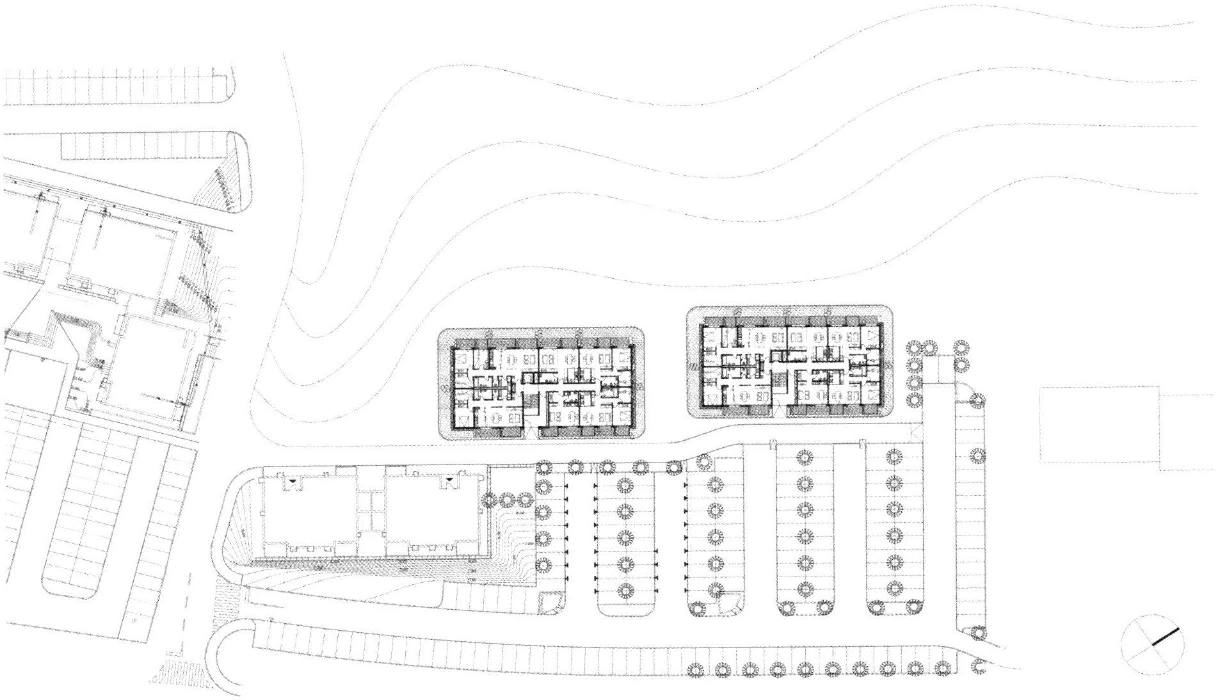

86

Windshape, 2006
Address: 24260 Lacoste, France. **Project partners:** SCAD students. **Client:** Savannah College of Art and Design (SCAD). **Materials:** plastic pipes, aluminum collars, white polypropylene string.

To twine together
ARCHITECTS: nARCHITECTS

Windshape was an ephemeral structure commissioned by the Savannah College of Art and Design as a venue and gathering space near their Provence campus. Built by nARCHITECTS and a team of SCAD students, it became the small town's main public meeting space, and hosted concerts, exhibitions, and ceremonies throughout the summer of 2006. The two eight-meter high pavilions dynamically changed with the Provencal wind. Fifty kilometers of white polypropylene string was threaded through the lattice to create swaying enclosures. The string was woven into dense regions and surfaces and pinched to define doorways, windows, and spaces for seating. The string responds to the wind in several ways by varying tension to create anything from rhythmic oscillations to fast ripples across its surfaces.

01 Worm's-eye view **02** Aerial view
03 Night view **04** Interior view **05**
Components diagram **06** Structure
diagram **07** Ondulated forms **08**
Interior by night

05

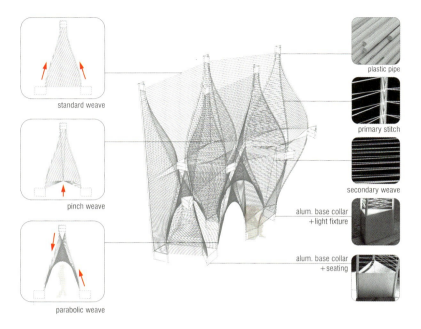

standard weave

pinch weave

parabolic weave

plastic pipe

primary stitch

secondary weave

alum. base collar
+light fixture

alum. base collar
+seating

06

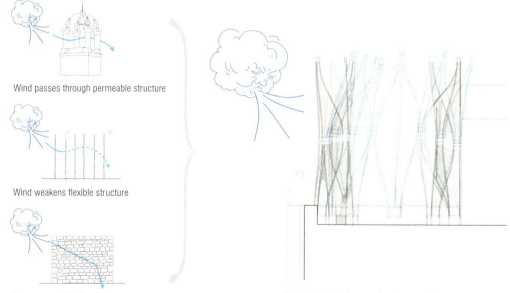

Wind passes through permeable structure

Wind weakens flexible structure

Opaque mass blocks wind

Supple+structural network registers wind

90

01

Lucciole, school complex, 2006
Address: 16–18, rue Edouard-Vallet, 1232 Cressy, Switzerland. **Client:** Communes of Bernex and Confignon, Geneva. **Gross floor area:** 6,042 m². **Materials:** concrete, steel, glass, fabric (shades).

Curtain wall

ARCHITECTS: dl-a, designlab-architecture sa.
Patrick Devanthéry and Inès Lamuniére

The buildings are placed in the middle of a new ensemble of residential houses. The three buildings are set apart from one another by virtue of a series of geometrical rotations creating intervening spaces that open into one another. Each of these three "objects" deposited upon their plateau of brushed concrete (a larger square volume, the school; a small cuboid volume, the assembly hall; a long semi-buried volume, the gymnasium) is enveloped by a double glass skin which ensures rational management of heat exchange. At night, this double skin lights up according to the result of the accumulated energy. Like four fireflies, their fluorescence epitomizes the lively character of this public space. Varicolored shades give the buildings a playful appearance.

03

01 Sunshades in the entrance area of the gym **02** Façades of gym and assembly hall **03** School, first floor plan **04** Situation plan **05 + 06** Color impressions during night

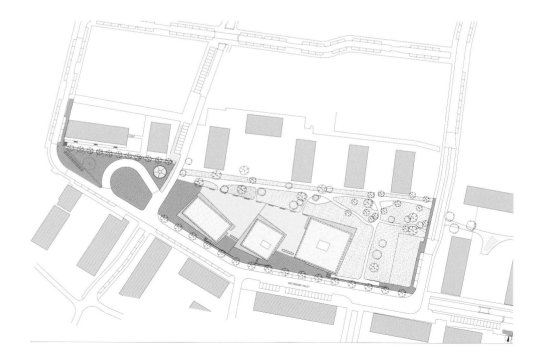

One room house Rupp, 2001
Address: Landstraße 112, 6971 Hard, Austria. **Client:** Petra Rupp. **Gross floor area:** 170 m². **Materials:** steel, white fir wood, fabric.

Elevated wooden box
ARCHITECTS: Architekturbüro Früh

This single house in the Hard community of eastern Austria is an elevated wooden box which appears to levitate above the large, leafy plot. A light steel structure makes up the outer framework of the unusual house and gives it the required ground contact. The wooden box of the residential story is on the upper level. The garage and additional functions are found in a markedly smaller cube located below. Externally, the building is structured using two different materials. A transparent skin of satined glass dominates the garage cube. Silver fir and sun shades made of textile dominate the module's façade. The shades add a needed dash of color to the building and hide the private spaces from peering eyes.

01

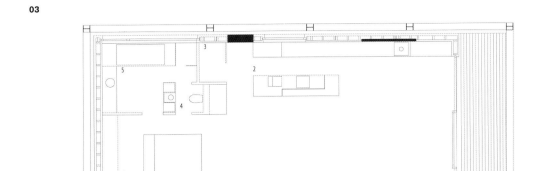

01 Balcony with textile sun shades
02 South-east elevation **03** Upper
floor plan **04** Section **05** View of
living area **06** North-west elevation
at dusk

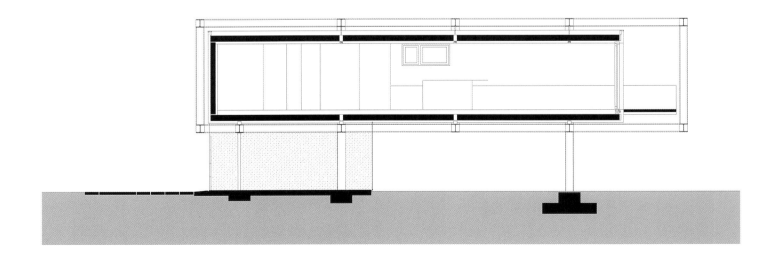

Residential house with jewelry studio, 2008
Address: Im Steinboß 11–13, 73550 Waldstetten-Wiß-
goldingen, Germany. **Structural engineers:** Dr. Ing.
Hottmann. **Client:** Georg Spreng. **Gross floor area:**
615 m². **Materials:** fabrics (curtain).

Exposed seclusion

ARCHITECTS: C18 Architekten
Marcus Kaestle, Andreas Ocker, Michel Roeder

This combined residence and studio presented a special challenge to the architects. Various uses as well as
exposed and private areas had to be placed in a relation to each other while simultaneously being separated
from one another. An interplay of different references
arising from the topography and requirements placed
on the building has resulted in a highly individual living
space. The building structure is dominated by clear geometrical forms interrupted and loosened up by opulent
outer drapes. In addition, the story-high draping enables
an open architecture with large-format glazings which
do justice to the fantastic views, while ensuring sufficient privacy.

01 Front elevation 02 Perspective
03 Curtains closed 04 Ground
floor plan 05 Basement floor plan
06 Perspective with pool

04

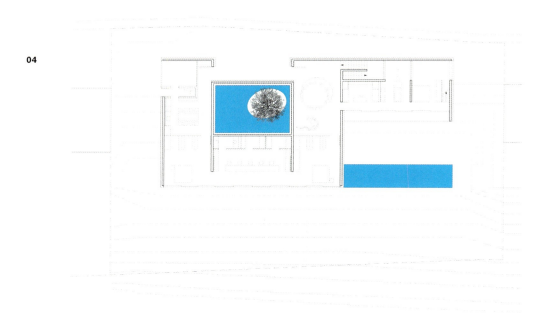

05

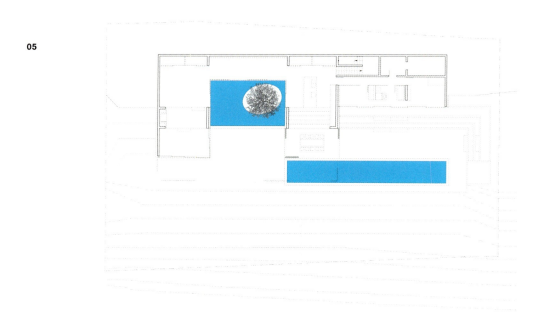

Hotel Ritter, 2008
Address: Im Tal 1, 77770 Durbach, Germany. **Client:**
Hotel Ritter – Family Müller. **Gross floor area:** 7,000 m².
Materials: apple wood, mix of traditional and contemporary materials, leather, wool.

Historic futurism

ARCHITECTS: JOI-Design interior architects

Starting in mid-2008 the hotel's appearance figures as
a bridge between tradition and modernity, and sparkles
thanks to the new lobby, bar and several restaurants,
as well as redesigned rooms and additional spa suites,
wellness areas and generous conference locations. A
silver knight's armor was placed between the lobby and
the passage to the bar. Various lounge furniture pieces
in brown and crème tones adapt to the older building
section. The consciously rowdy magenta-colored sofa
with a "granny" flower pattern creates a real eye catcher.
The spa area receives additional attention using textiles
in strong colors in its relaxation space which invite with
their overall form, color and materiality.

03

04

05

Sephora Shop, 2000
Address: Bercy Village, Paris, France. **Technical development:** Chaffik Gasmi and team. **Client:** Sephora. **Gross floor area:** 300 m². **Materials:** fabric for drapery and light sculptures.

Fine-flavored

ARCHITECTS: Jean-Marie Massaud

The design of the Sephora Shop located in the Bercy Village shopping mall in Paris makes extensive use of textiles to create a unique space experience. Fabrics are used in two different ways here: on the one hand, as a soft and folding veil that defines the circular shapes of the shopping areas, enclosing them like a soft garment, and on the other, as tensile lighting sculptures in the centers of each of the three circular spaces of round but clear forms. The stretched lighting sculptures provide a calm and soft illumination and accentuate the centers of each space, while the outer soft veil, also lit in colored tones, frames the sections in a playful manner. Different light impressions in addition with recurrent jar shapes throughout the whole place create an irrational spatial experience.

04

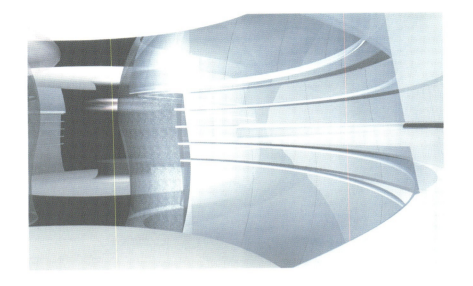

05

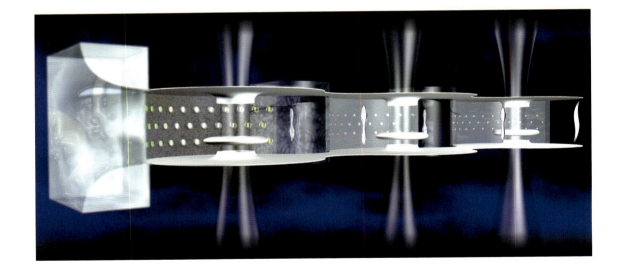

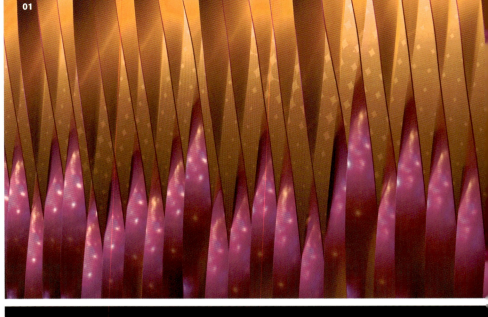

Jazzclub Bix, 2006
Address: Leonhardsplatz 28, 70182 Stuttgart, Germany. **Light design:** Candela Lichtplanung GmbH. **Acoustics:** Brüssau Bauphysik GmbH. **Structural engineers:** Zindel & Partner. **Client:** Jazzclub Stuttgart Betriebs GmbH, Jazzcom, City of Stuttgart. **Gross floor area:** 350 m². **Materials:** aluminum, fabrics.

(Un)jazzy colors

ARCHITECTS: Bottega + Ehrhardt Architekten

The new two-story jazz club is located in the listed Gustav Siegle House (Theodor Fischer, 1912, reconstruction by Martin Elsässer, 1954). A large auditorium for live Jazz performances on the ground floor and an intimate bar and lounge area on the upper level nest into each other. Both have a slightly angled bar to one side, which mirrors the non-orthogonal geometry of the house addition. A continuous wall panel creates a sense of identity and encompasses both the stage and the auditorium. Warm brown and gray tones as well as textile room partitions add density to the club atmosphere. Large-scale prints accent individual wall surfaces and a light object defines the double-height entrance area of the atmospheric room.

04

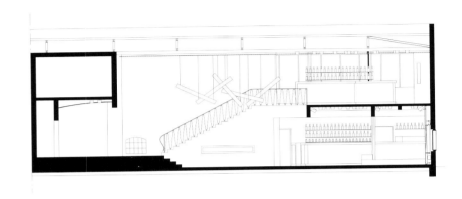

05

06

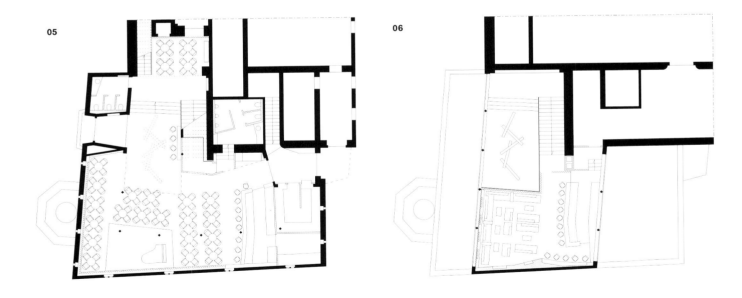

01

Light House Cinema, 2008
Address: Blackhall walk, Smithfield, Dublin 7, Ireland. **Client:** Light House Cinema & Fusano Properties. **Gross floor area:** 5,134 m². **Materials:** Quinnette Galley Cinema seats, black aluminum panels, american white oak timber, Kvadrat-Topas fabric.

Techniccolor

ARCHITECTS: DTA Architects
Dermot Reynolds + Colin Mackay

In refurbishing the Light House Cinema located within Smithfield Market, the architects took care to integrate a variety of screen sizes to ensure a diverse cinematic program and to be able to extend runs of popular films for longer periods. The architectural challenge of this project was to combine the insertion of four cinema volumes into existing basement voids, while creating an informal circulation route. Each of the four volumes has a consistent color coding which expresses the thematic diversity in accordance to the spatial structure and size of the rooms. Walls, furniture and floors were designed to optimize the cinematic experience while maintaining a unique character.

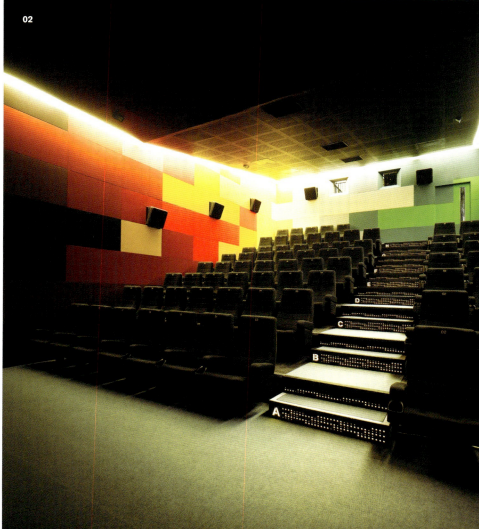

02

05

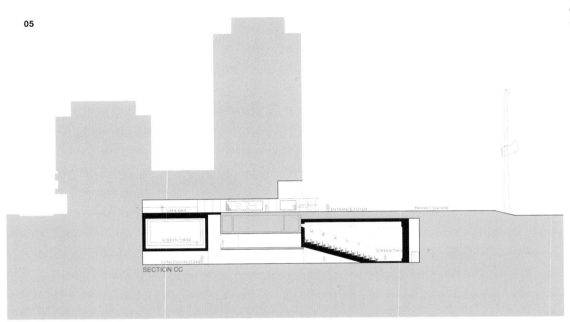

SECTION CC

06

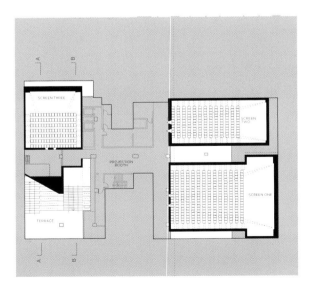

07

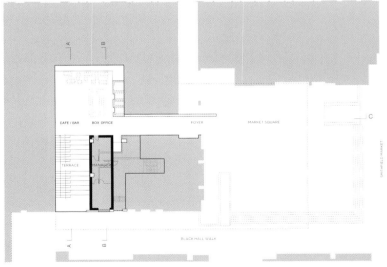

01

Kvadrat Sanden showroom, 2006
Address: Nackagatan 4, 116 41 Stockholm, Sweden.
Floors and furniture: Dinesen. **Client:** Kvadrat. **Gross floor area:** 250 m². **Materials:** textile partitions made of fabric "tiles".

Knit me a tile

ARCHITECTS: Ronan and Erwan Bouroullec

The Kvadrat showroom is structured using textile walls made of separate "tiles" assembled together via an ingenious folding system. The North Tiles system was conceived specifically for the textile showroom program. It aims to highlight various textures and materials featured in Kvadrat's collection by dressing the space with sensuality and warmth. It grants certain flexibility and guarantees a wide range of possible transformation. This system is the realization of long-incubated ideas about constructing soundproofed spaces with textile. Conceived similarly to fish scales, North Tiles can take on infinite shapes, both organic and geometric. The highly modular system allows the consideration of multiple applications for building autonomous and soundproofed locations.

02

04

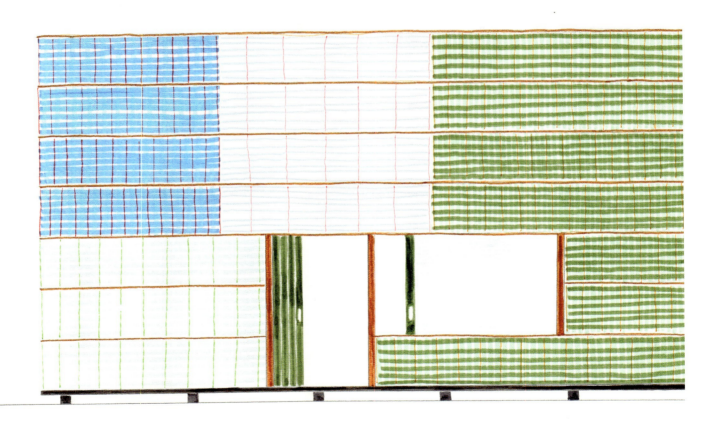

Shinagawa flat, 2006
Address: 4–14 Konan, Minato-ward, Tokyo 108-0075, Japan. **Client:** private. **Gross floor area:** 130 m². **Materials:** beige limestone, brown ceramic tiles, corian, robust fabric for carpet and sofa.

Geometric comfort

ARCHITECTS: Curiosity
Gwenael Nicolas

The concept for this apartment is based on the absence of walls and follows the clients' wish to create a space that is as open as possible. Space and function are structured by the use of differing materials. Living room, kitchen and bedroom are characterized by their specific floor treatment, each being selected for visual and functional qualities. The apartment thus awakes the impression that the separating walls have been removed, leaving the various treatments behind. The space's shape is also used to connect function: the form of the kitchen ceiling is visually linked to the dining table. In the upstairs bedroom and bathroom, a similar floor treatment for different room functions was used to create a rectangular space that appears larger than the sum of its functions.

03

04

01 Five different materials **02** The wellhole **03** 39th floor plan **04** 40th floor plan **05** Bird's-eye view from second floor

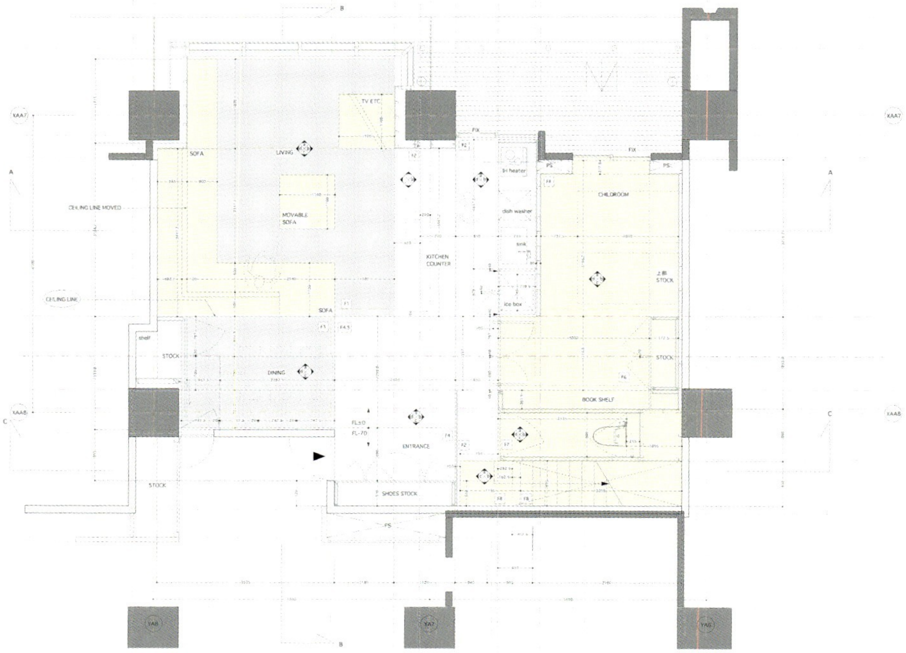

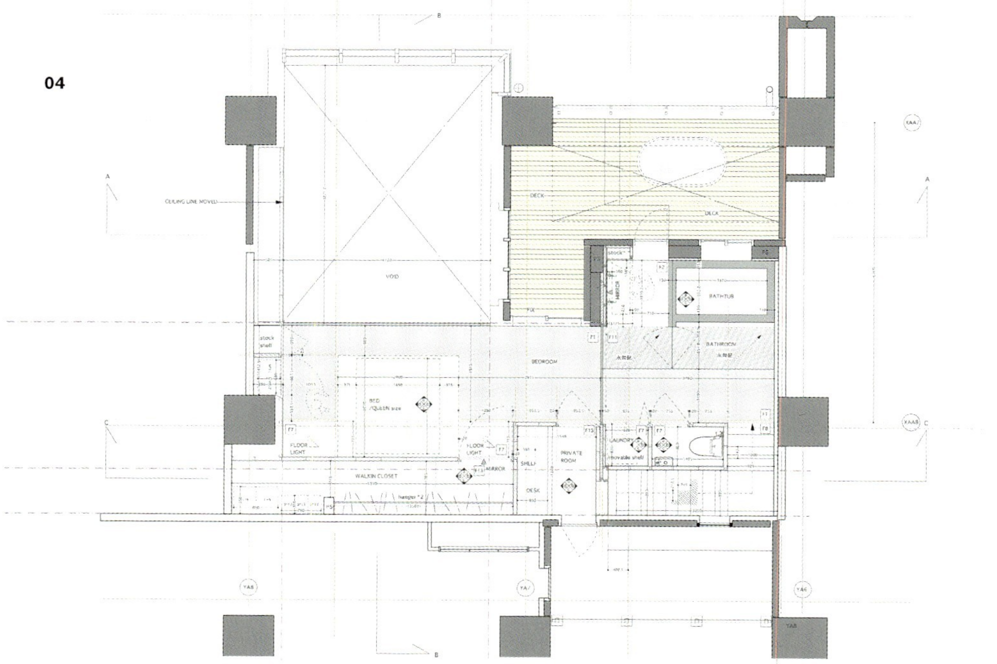

mini Bar, 2005
Address: City Hotel, Thielenplatz 2, 30159 Hanover, Germany. **Client:** Schreiber Projekt. **Gross floor area:** 180 m². **Materials:** red leather, floral patterned fabric for armchairs, wallpaper.

Grandma goes trendy

ARCHITECTS: JOI-Design interior architects

In the mornings, the integrated glass case invites with rolls and coffee, while at night the high bottle display of the back-lit bar summons guests for the cocktail hour. The color spectrum reaches from crimson red to coffee tones and includes black-and-white accents. A fresh yellow rounds off the color play and sets the stage for the bar. The material composition underlines the cult character of the existing building sections by using quotations from the past such as chandeliers in semitransparent cylinders, while flowery wall paper, which could have come out of an old kitchen drawer, gets a contemporary update thanks to its pompous dimensions and bright contrasting colors. Floral patterned armchairs quote wallpaper designs and are a definite eye draw.

01

03

St. Antonius church, 2006
Address: Burgstraße 29, 70569 Stuttgart-Kaltental, Germany. **Artist:** Madeleine Dietz. **Furniture:** pfeifer. kuhn. with Schreinerei Meister H.S. **Architects:** until 30.06.2005 pfeifer roser kuhn architekten. **Client:** Katholische Gesamtkirchenpflege Stuttgart. **Materials:** bunting of 100 % Trevira.

Trans-parament

ARCHITECTS: pfeifer. kuhn. architekten

The sparse, strict architecture of the small church designed by Hans Herkommer in 1932 makes it a monument, an example and a new challenge all in one. A canopy acting as a common roof rezones the house and marks the new center by referring to the Communio liturgy, staging a layout which at first appears as a contradiction. The canopy organizes various spatial elements, assigns the organ a new place along the axis and adds seating for mass goers parallel to the altar and ambo. In addition, it forms the central element for both natural and artificial illumination. Along with a new hypocaust floor, it also acts as an internal air collector which bundles solar energy and supplies the interior of the church in an economic fashion.

04

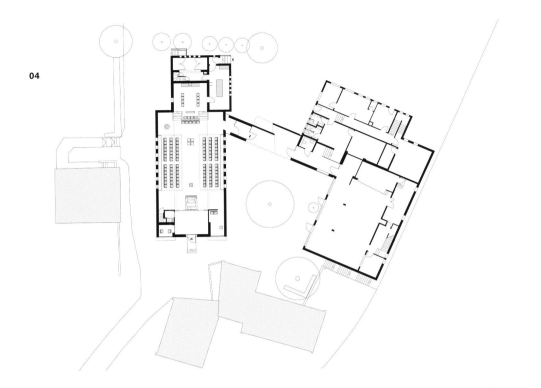

05

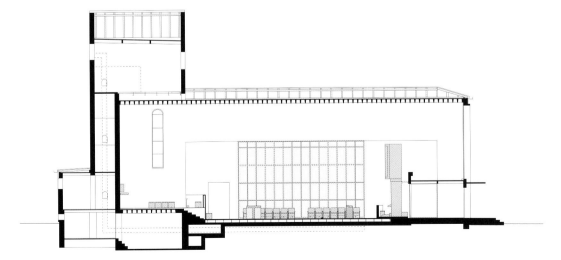

Schlafraum W, 2007
Address: Elsslergasse 26/5, 1130 Vienna, Austria.
Client: Jack Wagner. **Gross floor area:** 30 m². **Materials:** Curtain: version TISCA Soprano several colors; Leather: version WINTER, hand-waxed buffalo leather.

Dressed room

ARCHITECTS: epps architekten

It was the goal to create a sensual room from an existing bedroom inside a generous older apartment. This was achieved by using textiles and haptic materials. By being "dressed" in curtains, the room received a flowing drape which smoothes over all sharp contours. At the same time, the curtains hide all functional elements such as closets, doors and windows. The curtain rails sport various earthy tones. A special effect is created using a double-layered drape arrangement, resulting in a color play with a three-dimensional property. The bed is clad in hand-waxed buffalo leather, and harmonizes with the drape.

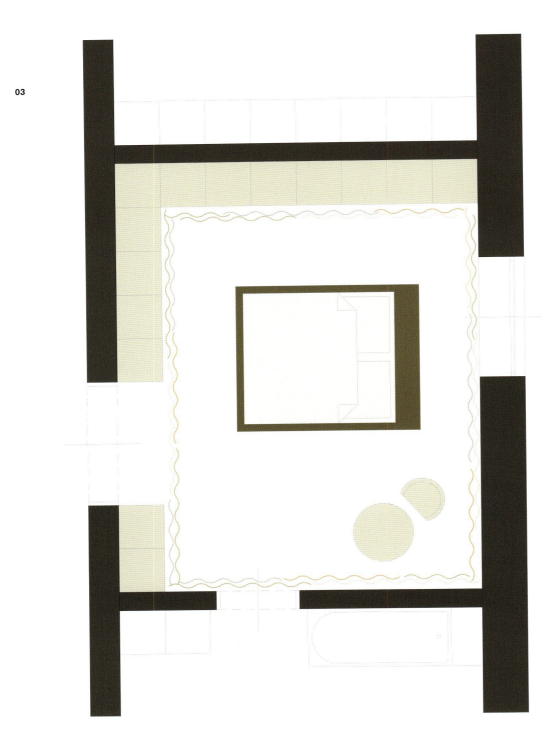

01 Detail **02** View towards window **03** Room plan **04** Bed and drapery

Kaufleuten Festsaal, 2006
Address: Pelikanplatz, 8001 Zurich, Switzerland.
Client: Kaufleuten AG. **Gross floor area:** 350 m².
Materials: walnut wood, different textures for acoustics, bronze, leather.

Velvet on the ground
ARCHITECTS: Pia M. Schmid

The ballroom in the businessmen's complex was erected in the 1920s by the business administrators' social club. The 350-square-meter room has been authentically restored and modernized, and hosts a range of events. The acoustically polished ballroom includes a bar, stage and gallery, and the reception area is buffered by a foyer. The historical space is now being revived for banquets, and for use as a lounge or bar with a dance floor. An impulsive composition using modern materials, intense and warm colors and an individually adjustable lighting concept have been combined with monument preservation details, leaving the historical ambience recognizable throughout the space. For example, the characteristic horizontal wall organization reverberates in the entire room.

01

03

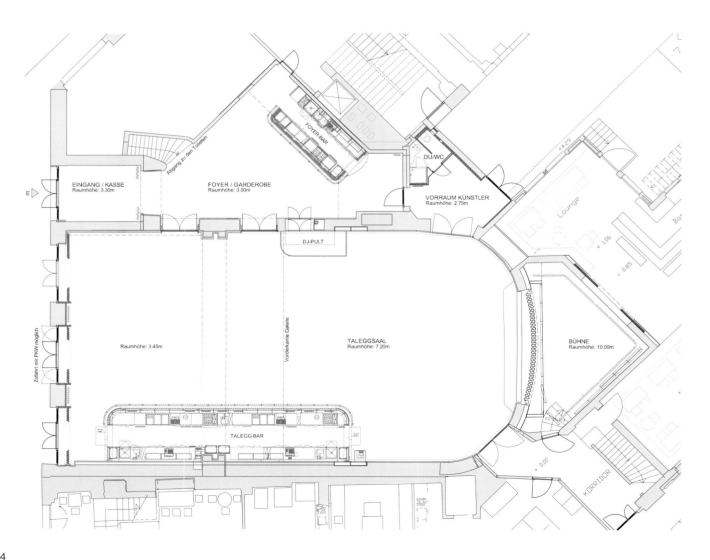

EINGANG / KASSE
Raumhöhe: 3.30m

Abgang zu den Toiletten

FOYER / GARDEROBE
Raumhöhe: 3.00m

FOYER-BAR

DU/WC

VORRAUM KÜNSTLER
Raumhöhe: 2.75m

Lounge

DJ-PULT

E

Zufahrt mit PKW möglich

Raumhöhe: 3.45m

Vorderkante Galerie

TALEGGSAAL
Raumhöhe: 7.20m

BÜHNE
Raumhöhe: 10.00m

+ 4.29

+ 1.06

+ 0.85

+ 0.00

TALEGG-BAR

KORRIDOR

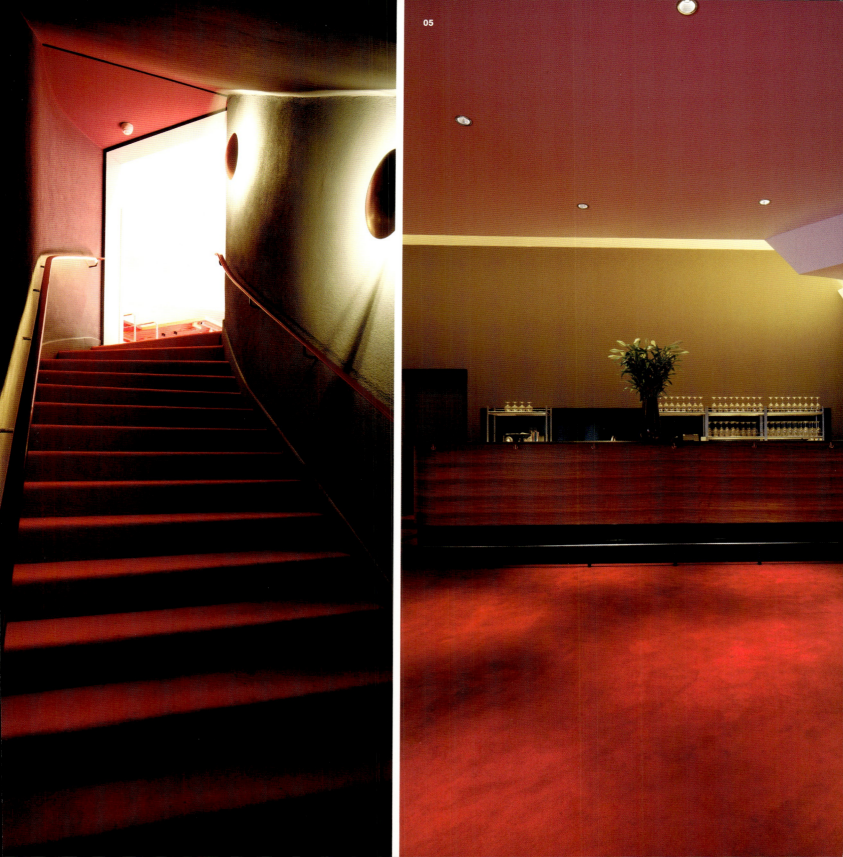

Hotel Missoni, 2009
Address: 1 George IV Bridge, Edinburgh EH1 1AD,
United Kingdom. **Architect:** Allan Murray Architects.
Creative director: Rosita Missoni. **Client:** Rezidor.
Gross floor area: 8,630 m². **Materials:** fabrics.

Quiet riot

ARCHITECTS: Matteo Thun & Partners

In the 8,630-square meter building in Edinburgh,
Matteo Thun & Partners worked on 129 rooms, seven
suites, the bar, restaurant and conference facilities
in close collaboration with Missoni. The name of this
prestigious Milan fashion house conjures up images
of a skilled use of many tones and shades: a minutely
applied, perfectly controlled riot of color. Used in tone
upon tone and tone against tone, the Missoni approach
to color gives its products an unmistakably strong
character of their own that is instantly recognisable the
world over. The designers developed a method to melt
Missoni's approach to their products with the interiors
of this outstanding hotel. The quality of the preparatory
thinking, the choice of materials and the final result
are every bit as painstaking as Missoni's own selec-
tions of color schemes.

01 Hotel room detail 02 Colorful drapery and furniture 03 Plan of hotel room 04 Variety of patterns

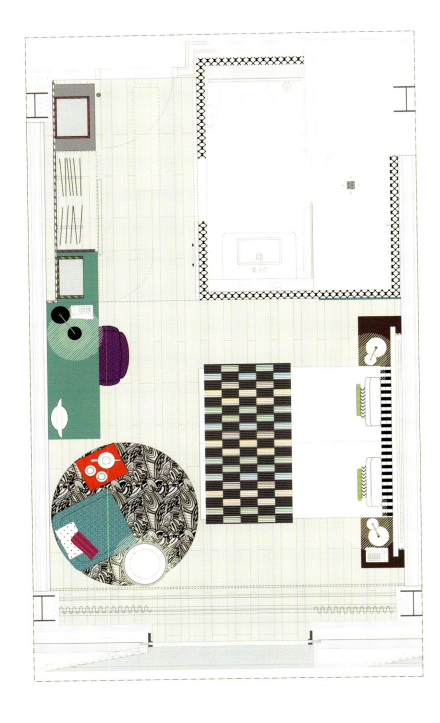

Nike iD Studio, 2005
Address: 255 Elizabeth Street, New York, 10012 NY, USA. **Artist:** Shiv. **Client:** Nike iD Studio. **Gross floor area:** 110 m². **Materials:** oiled walnut wood, lacquered steel, brushed aluminum, oiled ipe, cast resin.

Sweating out diamonds

ARCHITECTS: Lynch / Eisinger / Design

More lounge than showroom, the Nike iD Studio combines and reveals an inherent contradiction between luxury (sedentary, comfortable and elite) and athleticism (active, strenuous and egalitarian). This contradiction is a guiding principle behind the detailing of the space. Flocked wallpaper, seemingly stuffy and Victorian, is made up of sneakers and basketballs. Such visual puns are transposed to three dimensions, as wallpaper peels away from the walls to define seating areas below and a light cove above. No material stays in a single plane: walnut panels hover on one side of the space and then turn 90 degree into the room, taking the viewer's gaze with them. This implied sense of movement is everywhere, lending a sense of restlessness to the space.

04

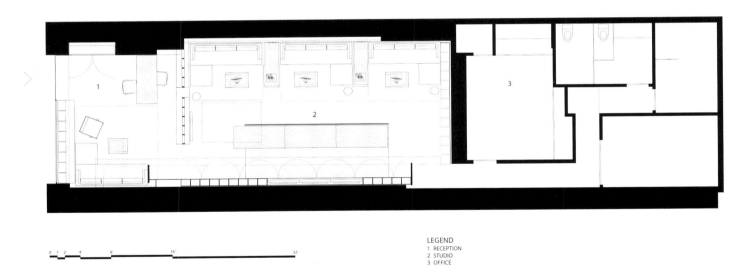

LEGEND
1 RECEPTION
2 STUDIO
3 OFFICE

Fifth Avenue apartment, 2006
Address: confidential. **Artist:** Rachel Lee Hovnanian.
Styling: Rianne Landstra. **Client:** private. **Gross floor
area:** 700 m². **Materials:** plastermoulding, oak floor,
limestone, fabrics.

Ebony and ivory

ARCHITECTS: Piet Boon Studio

This high-end Fifth Avenue apartment includes elements of European design. The client had in mind an
apartment where she could recover from her busy life
and the city's hectic tempo with her family. On the one
hand, the atmospheres to be evoked in each room were
defined beforehand, while on the other, the apartment
acts as a harmonious whole. The extraordinary works
of art by New York painter Rachel Lee Hovnanian con-
tribute to the meditative atmosphere. The most beauti-
ful fabrics are used to add to the serene ambiance,
making good use of natural light. Varied materials, or-
naments and forms are united using a consistent pal-
ette of black and white with a tender violet.

04

01 Hall way **02** Hall way with art work by Rachel Lee Hovnanian **03** Living room **04 + 05** Sketches **06** Living room with fireplace

05

Harisch Rutter offices, 2005
Address: Tegetthoffstraße 7, 1010 Vienna, Austria.
Lighting design: Christian Ploderer. **Client:** Büro
Harisch Rutter. **Gross floor area:** 450 m². **Materials:**
curtain, carpet, wood, covered doors, covered walls
with Alcantara.

Law & Order
ARCHITECTS: BEHF Architekten

The concept for the branch office of a law firm and
project development company was made subordi-
nate to the needs of later utilization. Consistent use
of select, high-quality materials creates a dense atmosphere, presenting itself malleable to the needs of
other users according to their discretion and image.
The rooms' textural and acoustic qualities answer to
the needs of sensitive and confidential interactions
with customers. All rooms maintain a discreet simplic-
ity, while all presentation and multimedia technology
is integrated in a way that effectively hides it. Large
mirrored surfaces continuously offer new vistas both
inside and out, breaking the perspective and even giving the corridor area spatial breadth and openness.

03

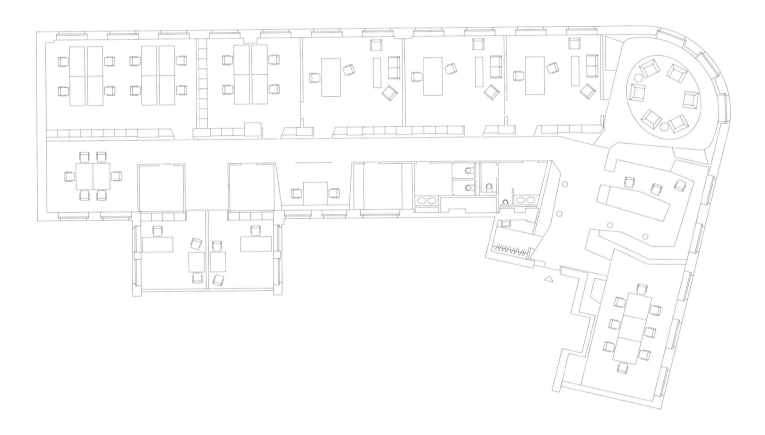

Le Meridien Parkhotel Frankfurt, 2007
Address: Wiesenhüttenplatz 28–38, 60329 Frankfurt/
Main, Germany. **Client:** Le Meridien/Starwood. **Gross
floor area:** 20,000 m². **Materials:** floral patterned
fabrics, white leather.

Old lady with a new gloss

ARCHITECTS: JOI-Design interior architects

In order to present the flagship hotel in the metropolis along the Main River in a new light, the interior of this stately building was completely refurbished in several stages. The classical façade leads the guest into a new, light lobby emanating warm elegance. Separate reception terminals greet each visitor individually. Walls upholstered in fine leather create the needed acoustic intimacy and simultaneously offer a pleasant haptic experience. Elegant colors such as mauve and beige interact with the dark parquet and brown carpet in the restaurant. This natural color cannon continues in the rooms and receives an additional color accent with the addition of blue details found in light and glass installations. This color play is further supported in the corridors.

01

01 Detail of hotel room **02 + 03** Different hotel rooms, total view **04** Plan of hotel room **05** Sketch of hotel restaurant **06** Leather and fabric surfaces in the lobby

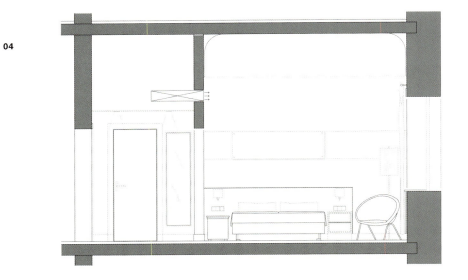

Google's EMEA Engineering Hub, 2008
Address: Brandschenkenstrasse 110, 8002 Zurich, Switzerland. **Client:** Google Inc. **Gross floor area:** 12,000 m². **Materials:** leather, different kinds of fabrics.

Code the puck

ARCHITECTS: Camenzind Evolution

The design of Google's Engineering Hub cultivates an energized and inspiring work environment which is relaxed but focused and buzzing with activities on seven stories for up to 800 staff. The Googlers participated in a tailor-made design process to create their own local identity and decided to reduce their personal net area of workspace in order to gain more communal and meeting areas. There are informal meeting areas, with a relaxed atmosphere for teams to have creative discussion around white-boards. Some of them incorporate the theme of the floor, like the Igloo Satellite Cabins with penguins and the original ski-gondolas in a snow-scape on the blue floor. Work and play are not mutually exclusive in this office, or as Google puts it, "it is possible to code and pass the puck at the same time".

04

05

Citizen service center of Innsbruck-Land, 2008
Address: Gilmstraße 2, 6020 Innsbruck, Austria.
Client: District Innsbruck-Land. **Gross floor area:**
465 m². **Materials:** serigraphy printed textiles of
low flammability.

Messages on the wall

ARCHITECTS: Hannes Hunger
ARTISTS: Evelyn Grill, Elke Salzmann (tex art)

In order to optically enlarge the room on the ground
floor of the Innsbruck local administration building,
architect Hannes Hunger has equipped the skylight
reflector surfaces with an underlying artistically decorated textile acoustic wall, which is perceived as a
space divider. In this public service area, cool (fair-
faced concrete) and warm (textile) material surfaces
were consciously selected for the public service area
and invigorated with the help of a rainbow glass wall
illumination. Evelyn Grill, a textile artist, made use of
an experimental screenprinting technique to add a
painterly touch to the overall appearance of the im-
posing acoustic wall. A landscape of soft color tran-
sitions continuing over the entire length of the wall
was created thanks to the combination of typographic
elements and oval shapes.

03

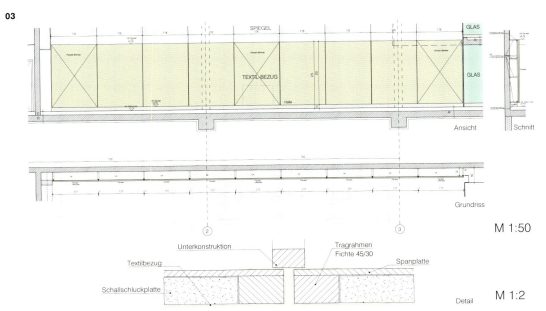

SPIEGEL

GLAS

TEXTIL-BEZUG

GLAS

Halle

Ansicht

Schnitt

Grundriss

M 1:50

Unterkonstruktion

Tragrahmen
Fichte 45/30

Textilbezug

Spanplatte

Schallschluckplatte

Detail   M 1:2

04

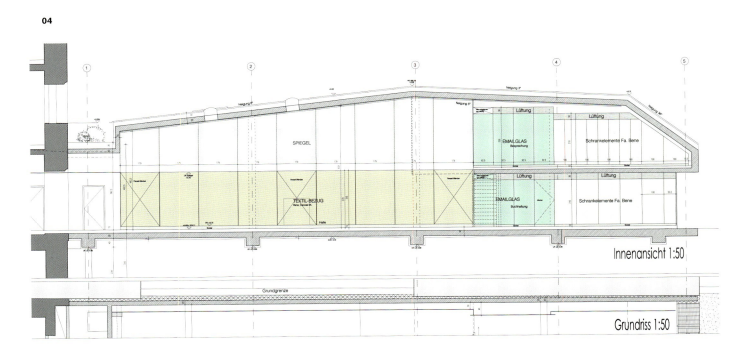

Neigung 3°

Lüftung

Lüftung

SPIEGEL

EMAILGLAS
Besprechung

Schrankelemente Fa. Bene

Lüftung

Lüftung

TEXTIL-BEZUG

EMAILGLAS
Buchhaltung

Schrankelemente Fa. Bene

Halle

Innenansicht 1:50

Grundgrenze

Grundriss 1:50

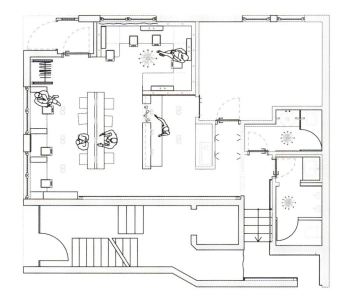

Gerberei, 2007
Address: Christophstraße 14, 70178 Stuttgart, Germany. **Planning partner:** Tobias Petri. **Client:** C. Wenzelburger. **Gross floor area:** 80 m². **Materials:** cement, concrete, polyurethane foam, leather.

Delicate skin
ARCHITECTS: planungsbüro i21
Heiko Gruber

"Good things come in small packages" is the motto for the refurbishment of this bar. Located in a former tanners' quarter, the name Tannery and the associated main material, leather, were quickly settled upon. The floor was treated with a four-millimeter thick layer of a cement-like material. A leather wall, which was variously upholstered, dominates the space and serves as a large backrest, table complement and furniture element used for presentation. Upholstered seating was manufactured using polyurethane foam and is sturdy and soft, like leather. Guiding systems with a leathery feel and indirect illumination lead the guest through the bar. Themed areas were created in the sanitary stations: golden surfaces with layered material sparkle in the ladies' room in contrast to the black tones greeting the gents.

01 Floor plan **02** Perspective showing functional desk and leather wall **03** Seating area **04** Detail of leather wall

Susana Solano Exhibition, 2008
Address: Museo Colecciones ICO, Zorrilla, 28014 Madrid, Spain. **Client:** ICO Foundation. **Gross floor area:** 1,500 m². **Materials:** paper.

Wrapping paper
ARCHITECTS: Cadaval & Sola-Morales Arquitectos

The project aims to scale the space to the size of the objects to be displayed here, providing order and rhythm to an exhibition which aims to be intimate. The models of public sculptures done by Susana Solano are treated as jewels that relate to each other visually as they do historically. A single system is designed to suit two spaces with opposed spatial attributes, allowing for a single reading of the exhibit. A unique envelope ought to unify spatial perception while solving by its layout the display of the pieces. A fragile, translucent, white, almost sacramental envelope is build to receive a number of sturdy and powerful pieces. The reference is clear: the paper lamps used in fairs, made out of a fragile honeycomb paper, with its volume build up on air and inventiveness.

01 Interior view 02 Corner 03, 04
Honeycomb structure 05 Elevation
06 Ground floor plan 07 Perspective 08 Elevation with art by Susana
Solano

05

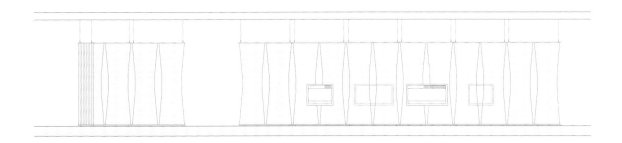

06

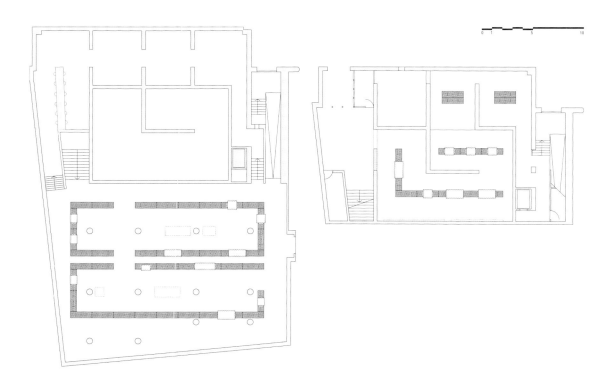

Sports center, 2008
Address: Bistrupvej, 3460 Birkerød, Denmark.
Planning partners: Schmidt, Hammer & Lassen
Architects. **Client:** Birkerød Municipality. **Gross floor
area:** 9,200 m². **Materials:** fiberglass, fabrics.

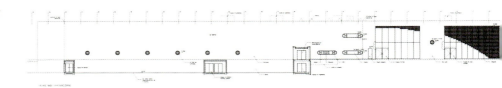

The modern curtain
DESIGNER: Astrid Krogh Design

The façades of this newly completed sports and leisure
complex with a distinctive sculptural quality were designed by Schmidt, Hammer & Lassen and the Dan-
ish artist Astrid Krogh and are an example of a close
collaboration between artist and architect. Black circles
form interlinking patterns when the louvers are closed,
with the translucent cladding adding a glowing quality to
the daylight filtering through it to the interior. The structure consists of fiberglass panels, whose strength allows them to be made to very thin specifications. More-
over, the composite can be glued to the glazing without
clunky mullions and transoms while avoiding friction
between glass and frame. Vertical louvers can be drawn
to one side and locked in the open or closed position in
order to regulate light.

01 Elevation **02** View by night **03 + 04** Interior view

01

KT: the listening room, 2008
Address: Meiji-jingu-gaien, 2-3 Kasumigaokamachi, Shinjyuku-ward, 160-0013, Tokyo, Japan. **Planning partners:** Lou Weis, Freek Dech. **Client:** Tokyo Designer's Week. **Gross floor area:** 18 m². **Materials:** corrugated fiberboard, extruded polystyrene.

Music in the air

ARCHITECTS: mat studio, elastik

KT: the listening room attempts to create a personal audio experience in a secluded and private space in the turmoil of a high-profile design event in the heart of Tokyo. CNC-sliced corrugated fiberboard and extruded polyester foam panels are systematically clustered to form a circle of speakers, all focally oriented towards the listener's sofa. The material and acoustic design are intertwined into a whole, where principles of soundproofing, reflectivity, rigidity and channeling of the reverberation are taken into account. The listening position of a visitor to the KT container is acoustically isolated, while the visual connection with the outside is retained. The distinction between acoustics, structure and ornament fade into a singular integrated personal space.

02

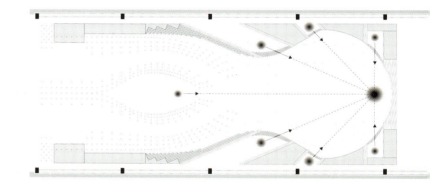

03

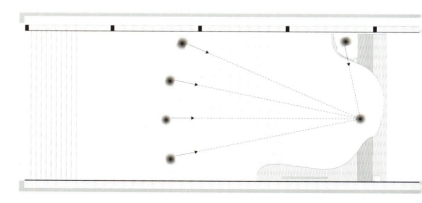

01 Axonometry of listening room **02** Ground floor plan **03** Section **04** Interior of listening room

ROC Care & Health, 2007
Address: Laan van de Mensenrechten 500, 7331 VZ Apeldoorn, The Netherlands. **Planning partners:** Kunst en Bedrijf. **Client:** ROC Apeldoorn. **Gross floor area:** 250 m². **Materials:** wood, carpet, leather, bisonyl.

Hospitality
ARCHITECTS: Tjep.

The designers were asked by the ROC Professional Training School in Apeldoorn in The Netherlands to design the reception area of the Care & Health Department. The idea of care has been visualized in a humoristic way using different interior elements. A protective shelter in the shape of a large box with a seemingly swung open cover forms a relaxation area. The interior surfaces of the shelter are covered with fabric reminiscent of oriental carpets. Tidy made-up beds become chairs. The reception desk is formed by soft mattresses and an informal meeting space is created by simply protecting a table by a sick bay tent. In their sum, these elements create a funny kind of hospitality as a result of their juxtaposition with hospitals.

02

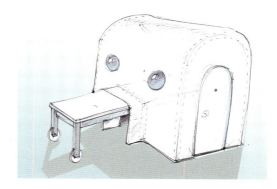

03

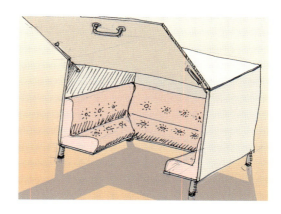

01 Tent interior **02** Sketch of tent **03** Sketch of shelter **04** Reception desk with tent in the background **05** Shelter with seating furniture

ACCESSORY

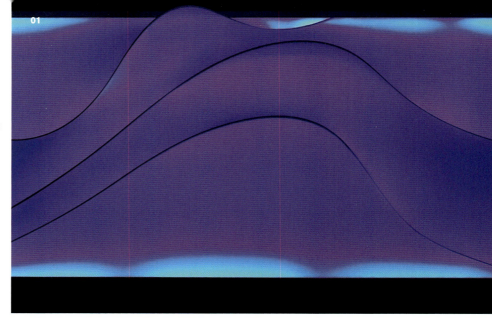

01

Lightform panels, 2007
Address: 3667 Las Vegas Boulevard S, Las Vegas, NV 89109, USA. **Interior design:** Dougall Design Associates. **Lighting:** CD+M Lighting Design Group. **Client:** Planet Hollywood Resort and Casino. **Gross floor area:** 93 m². **Materials:** fiberglass, inherently flame resistant polyester/lycra fabric.

Dancing walls
ARCHITECTS: Studio Lilica

Studio Lilica's Lightform panels are a series of five framed and backlit fabric sculptures constructed of inherently fire-resistant polyester/lycra material that is stretched over a system of free-form fiberglass ribs. The project was commissioned by the interior design firm Dougall Design Associates for the Planet Hollywood Resort and Casino in Las Vegas. The sculptural panels were designed as a field of curved planes that creates a shifting landscape of light. The use of fabric allows the sculpture's contours to weave in and out of the picture plane, creating a topography of light and shadow. The panel series was designed so that each individual panel could stand on its own or flow into the others to complete the series. CD+M Lighting Design Group designed the computerized color-changing lighting system.

02

01 Panel purple **02** Panel **03** Panel series pink **04** Panel series green

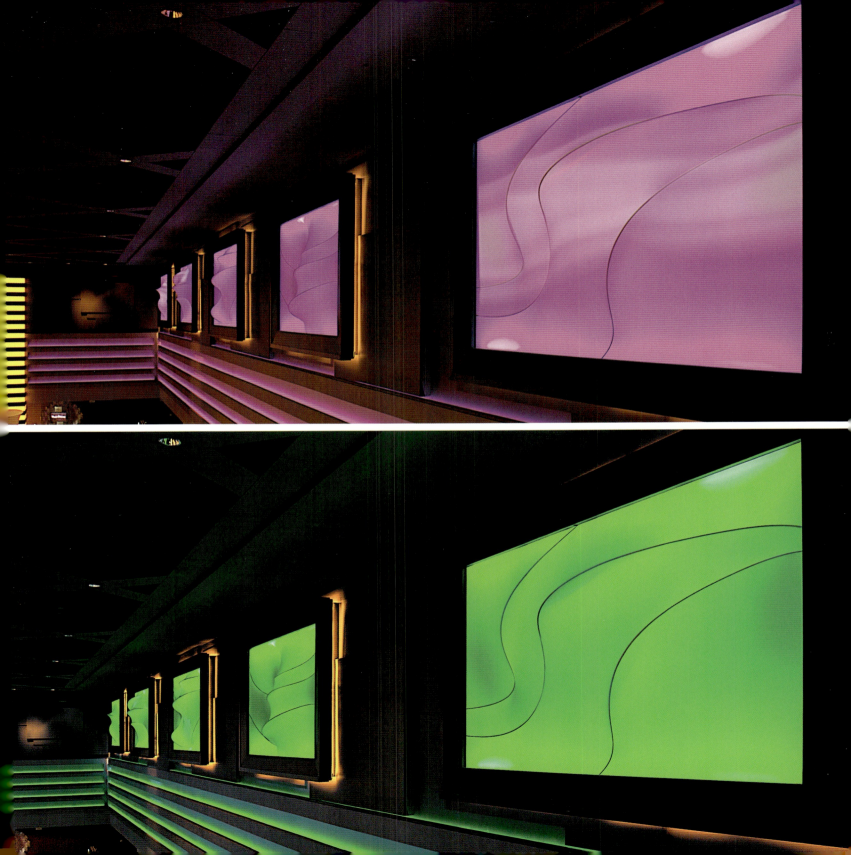

The Clouds, 2008
Materials: fabric partitions (Kvadrat).

Bit by bit

ARCHITECTS: Ronan and Erwan Bouroullec

The Clouds are made of similar elements attached by special rubber bands. They have been designed to be used in a range of different applications from the decorative screen to the sound absorbing wall and produce a unique three-dimensional effect, coating architecture in a both fluid and somehow chaotic way. Single elements can be added to the mainframe and let the object itself constantly evolve. Simple configuration and modularity of the structures allows for free arrangement and rearrangement of the single tiles until the intended effect and shape is achieved. Used as a large scale installation in hotels, offices or shops, they can offer a more human space bringing surprisingly colorful fabric windows to the place that can be altered in shape and color if there is a need for change.

04

Field of Play, 2006
Address: One Manhattan Square, Rochester, NY 14607, USA. **Planning partners:** Scott Eberle. **Fabricator fabric structures:** Transformit. **Client:** Strong National Museum of Play. **Gross floor area:** 650 m². **Materials:** aluminum tube frame structure, machined aluminum connections, Polyester spandex fabric.

Playtime

ARCHITECTS: Strong National Museum of Play
Matthew Handy

Field of Play explores the nature and importance of play, and its benefits to individuals and society. Four areas contain fabric elements: In the toddler "aquarium," translucent fabric structures lit with color-changing LEDs mimic the stream of evanescent light coming from the ocean's surface. In the drawing activity area, a fabric structure serves as a projection screen. In the music area, striking the spinning xylophones causes colored lights to wash across the fabric sculptures above, inspiring musical and visual play between guests. In the theater area, a large tension fabric header is backlit by color-changing lights which highlight its structure. This structure is shaped like a jigsaw puzzle, a reference to the museum's collection of toys, games, and play-related artifacts.

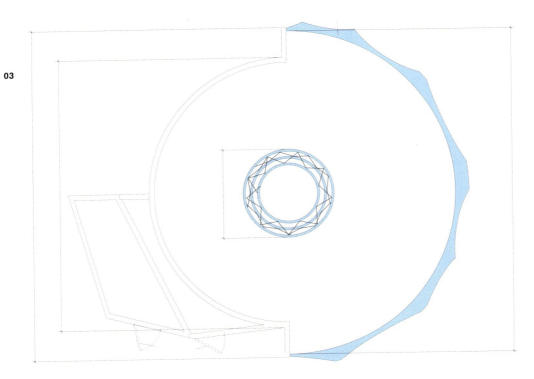

03

01 The toddler "aquarium" **02** Theater header with fabric tensile structure **03** Plan of theater **04** Concepts for fabric sculpture above a spinning xylophone **05** Illuminated fabric sculptures

04

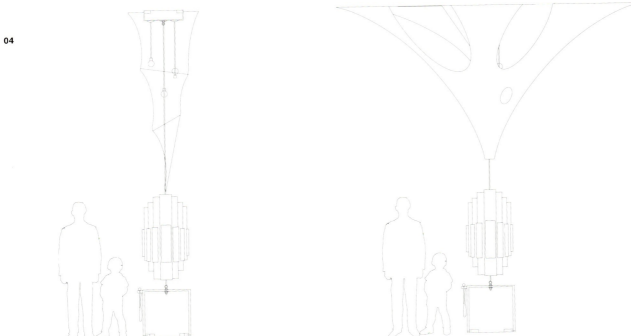

196

Pier at Caesars, Caesars Palace, 2006
Address: One Atlantic Ocean, Atlantic City, NJ 08401, USA. **Project architects:** Elkus Manfredi Architects. **Fabricator:** Eventscape Inc. **Lighting design:** Focus Lighting Inc. **Client:** Caesars Atlantic City Casino & Hotel. **Gross floor area:** 53,420 m². **Materials:** light-weight double curved aluminum frames with flexible fabric membrane covering.

Walk on water

DESIGNERS: Rockwell Architects

A dramatic addition to Caesars Palace, this three-story, 100-shop, high-end retail facility extends 457 meters directly out into Atlantic Ocean. The Pier features an Eventscape element, where framed fabric panels float suspended from the ceiling, evoking the clouds and waves of the seascape. Soothing waves of light projected onto the ceiling structures create the illusion of a relaxing stroll along the beach. The use of fabric was an ideal solution as the custom undulating wave panels could not have been made using traditional building methods. These panels create a tranquil mood which invites lingering in fascinating shops, and adds a lively rhythm to a very long straightaway.

01

03

04

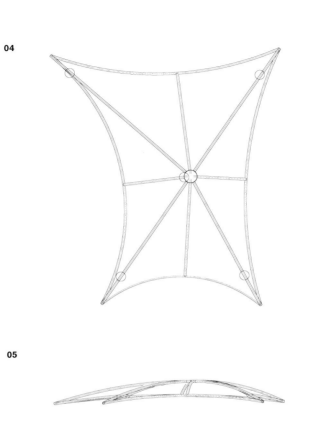

05

06

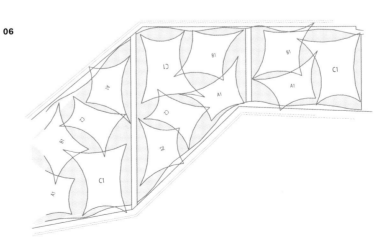

01

Levitating Archives, 2006
Address: Am Sandtorkai 68–70, 20457 Hamburg, Germany. **Planning:** üNN (Rolf Kellner). **Sculpture:** Jens J. Meyer. **Projection:** Katrin Bethge. **Client:** HafenCity Hamburg, Hamburgische Kulturstiftung, Körber-Stiftung. **Gross floor area:** 26 m, 20 m x 12 m. **Materials:** Lashing: LIROS PES, PP; Fabric: cotton/spandex.

Reminiscences in the hourglass
ARCHITECTS: Rolf Kellner
ARTISTS: Jens J. Meyer, Katrin Bethge

This installation in Hamburg's HafenCity is based on white drapery elements forming a complex sculpture which fills the space with light, lightness and motion. The network of drapes has been integrated into the existing architecture and levitates between the structures. Historical and current images are projected on the sails with the descent of darkness, transforming them into floating witnesses of history as well as current events. Past and present are examined thanks to the textile installation, letting the fragmentary nature of our perception be experienced. No other material would have allowed this complex and unique projection surface to come about with such lightness.

02

Snow (as part of Tokyo Wonder Exhibition at Salone Internazionale del Mobile), 2008
Address: La Posteria, Via Giuseppe Sacchi n5/7, 20121 Milan, Italy. **Client:** TONERICO:INC. **Gross floor area:** 29.5 m². **Materials:** acid etching polyester.

Let it snow, let it snow ...
ARCHITECTS: TONERICO:INC.
Hiroshi Yoneya, Ken Kimizuka, Yumi Masuko

This spatial installation was presented at the gallery in Milan during Salone Internazionale del Mobile. The "SNOW" was located on the corridor space linking the entry and the back of gallery space. Patterned, translucent fabrics are suspended at equal intervals. The layers create an impression of snow falling inside the exhibition space. White color spreads over the surroundings and purifies day-to-day scenes. The corridor serves as a sluice between the exterior and the interior, provoking a similar movement for the visitors on the emotional level. The material is thin and light, is swayed by the movement of the air and generates the atmosphere of frailty and transience, countering our search for rigidity and steadiness.

03

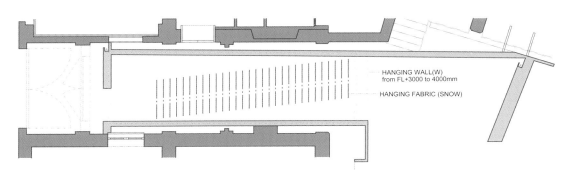

HANGING WALL(W)
from FL+3000 to 4000mm

HANGING FABRIC (SNOW)

04

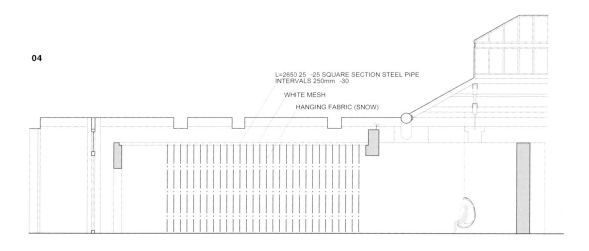

L=2650 25 –25 SQUARE SECTION STEEL PIPE
INTERVALS 250mm –30

WHITE MESH

HANGING FABRIC (SNOW)

Softhousing, 2003
Address: Venables Street, 1470, V5L 2G7, Vancouver, Canada. **Materials:** paper, polyethylene fibre.

Concertina

ARCHITECTS: molo
Stephanie Forsythe and Todd MacAllen

Softhousing was the original concept that launched molo's innovative and award-winning family of expandable / compressible honeycomb structures called "soft". The main thought behind "soft" is the creation of flexible and spontaneous space, the ability to temporarily shape more intimate ephemeral areas within larger open spaces, and return the space to the larger room when needed. Using simple lightweight sheets of humble materials such as paper and non-woven textiles, the honeycomb geometry results in structures of high strength and flexibility while using building materials in an economical fashion. A collection of flexible space making elements from softhousing has sprung to life, including seating, lighting and a modular system of walls and building blocks with seamless magnetic connections.

02

08

Entry off public corridor

Plywood storage cabinet

Flexible honeycomb structure private rooms
in three possible positions
anchored to plywood cabinets at wall

Laundry

Sink

Tiolet

Table

Bath

Flexible honeycomb walls

Kitchen

Sliding glass doors

Balcony (engawa)

Translucent glass louvers (operable)

N

AA

BB

09

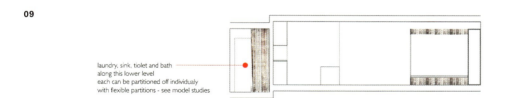

laundry, sink, tiolet and bath
along this lower level
each can be partitioned off individualy
with flexible partitions - see model studies

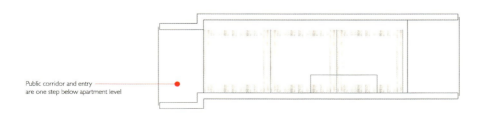

Public corridor and entry
are one step below apartment level

213

Sinus drapery, 2006
Address: anywhere. **Gross floor area:** 20 m². **Materials:** plastic covered steel, wool felt.

Sinful sinus curves

DESIGNERS: Johanna Lindgren Örn and Helen Högberg

Sinus is a space with a sound absorbing function created using industrial wool felt elements vertically suspended on wires. The wavy felt sections allow generous daylight penetration and create a nice, quiet space which is visually connected to its surroundings. Sinus drapery presents a possibility to easily divide larger spaces into smaller units without the use of heavy walls. The designers strongly believe that soft materials make interactions between people and spaces more human, and have proved that textiles can play a crucial role in architecture with the hope that the material's influence will increase in the near future.

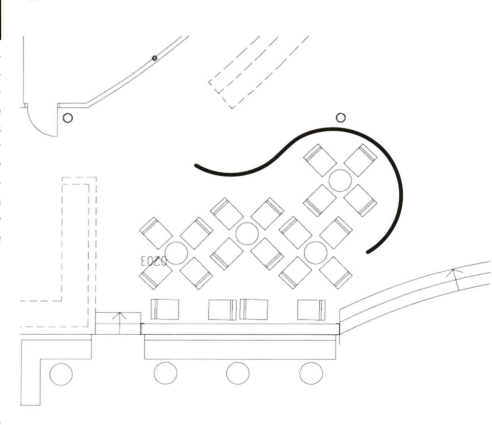

01 Sinus installation at Clarion Hotel **02** Plan **03** Sinus installed at Stockholm Furniture Fair

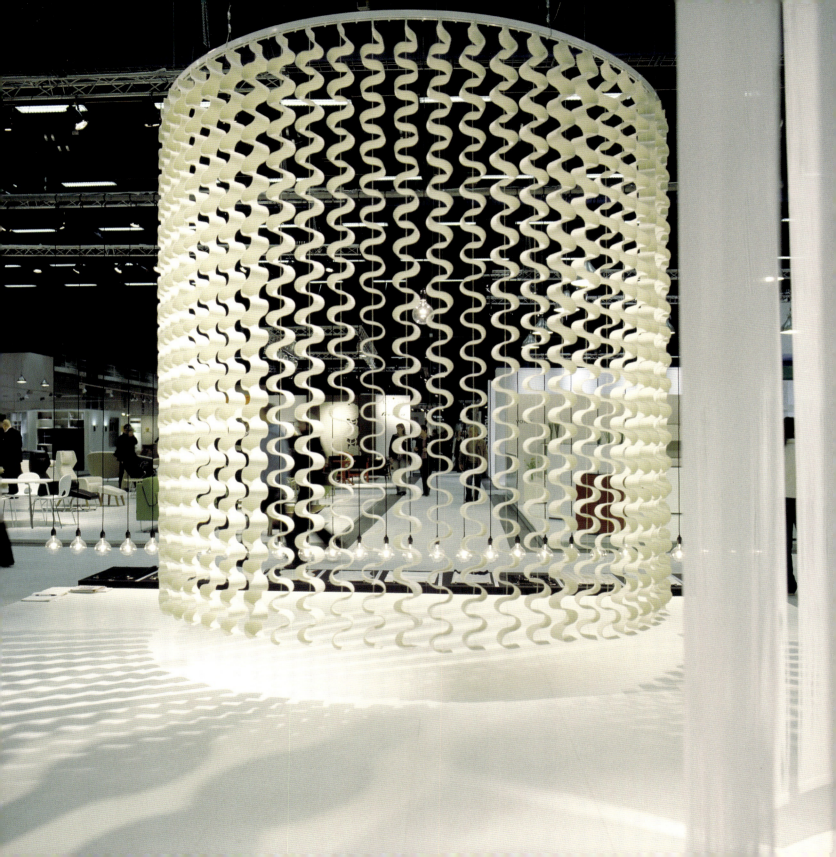

01

Showroom Barcelona, 2008
Address: Main hall, Moll Espanya, Barcelona, Spain.
Client: Clarity Spain. **Gross floor area:** 78 m². **Materials:** transparent nylon threads.

Sprightly wall

ARCHITECTS: ex.studio
Iván Juárez + Patricia Meneses

Thread, the basic element of the dress, creates space in this showroom. The intervention forms a transparent space that it is generated using light. It is delimited by multiple transparent threads which vary in their appearance throughout the day due to different light reflections. It resembles an ethereal vertical sculpture created by "sewing" the space through an artisan process. The vertical woven textile acts as a diluted glazed wall, suggesting inner and outer space without defining either. The boundary remains diaphanous, permeable and dynamic. A complex and delicate process was completed to realize the project. Three thousand nylon threads were placed five centimeters from each other on a suspended structure 13 meters in height.

02

05

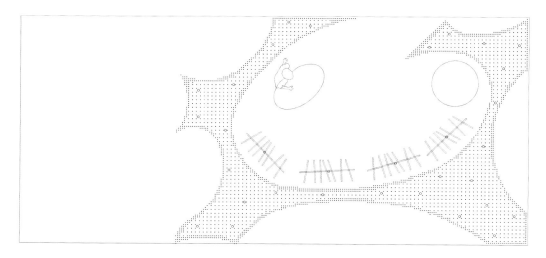

06

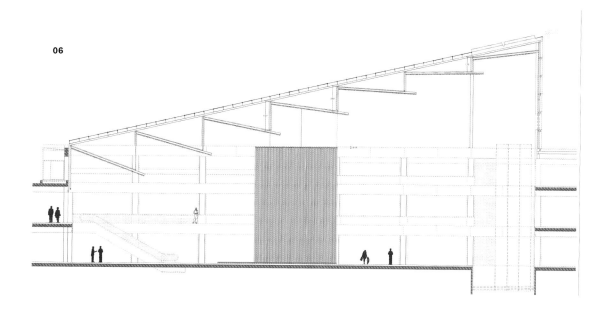

218

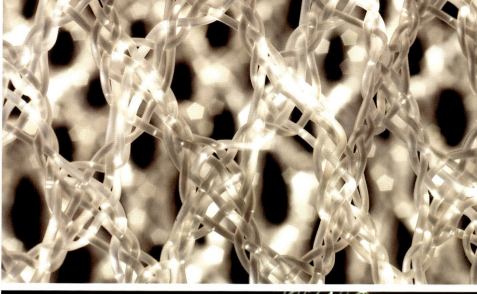

Bobbin Lace Lamp, 2006
Address: De Raadstraat 28K, 5666 EA Geldrop, The
Netherlands. **Client:** SKOR / Diaconessenhuis Leiden.
Materials: fiberglass.

The grace of lace

ARCHITECTS: Studio Van Eijk & Van der Lubbe

The Bobbin Lace Lamp, installed in the atrium of a hospital in Leiden, is a hand-knotted fiberglass construction
which can be customized for specific uses. No bulbs are
needed because light is transported through the fiberglass. The lamp shade becomes the actual light source,
inverting the common concept of a lamp. The strands,
each containing 400 filaments, were deliberately bro-
ken to let light seep through them to create a glowing effect. Shapes and configuration of the three lights
were inspired by surrounding geometrical forms.

04

05

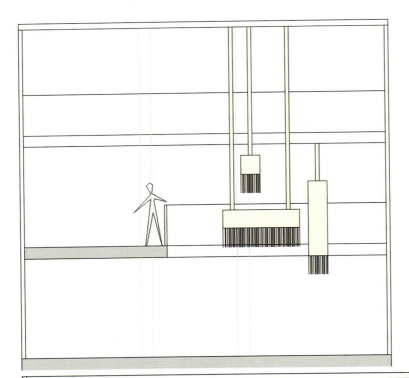

Exibition "Pixel um Pixel – edelweiss Stickerei", 2008
Address: TUCHINFORM, Obere Kirchgasse 8, 8400
Winterthur, Switzerland. **Materials:** yarn, cotton,
silk, linen, net lace.

Dpi

DESIGNERS: Ursula Spicher-Waldburger

Pixel by Pixel is an exhibition of embroidery art by
Ursula Spicher-Waldburger. The artist finds inspiration
in nature – the creative process begins with brush and
paper, and is further digitally developed using graphic
programs. Just as computer graphics are created using
pixels, the mesh forms of the embroidered textiles also
create pixilated patterns. Similar to pointillist art, the
panels exercise their effect only from a distance. This
way, the artist gives new forms to traditional arts using
new media and a strong creativity.

02

04

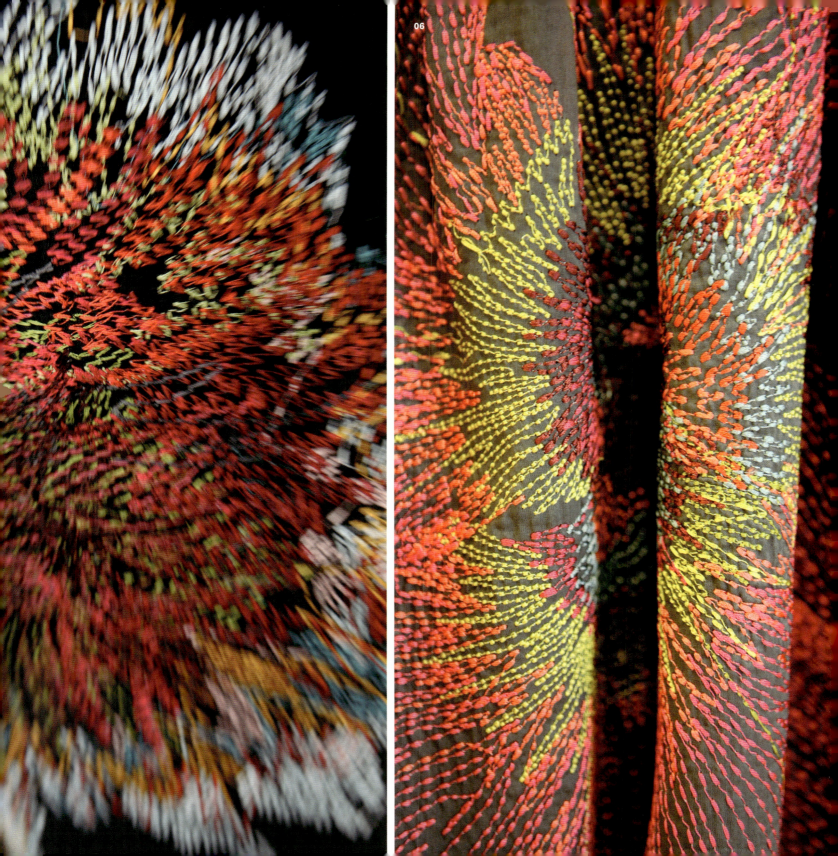

Livingstones, 2005
Materials: Neo-livingstones (exterior): neoprene, poly-silicone fibers, polyurethane; Livingstones (interior): Bultex foam rubber, polysilicone fibers, pure wool.

Soft as pebbles

ARCHITECTS: smarin

Livingstones is a series of textile furniture elements inspired by natural aesthetics. The series started with stone-shaped cushions reminiscent of pebbles which could be combined to individual organized rest areas capable of varying in size and shape. Bit by bit, some new elements like the Livingstones sofa and neo-Livingstones outdoor furniture joined the collection. Nowadays, one can choose between pebbles in various shapes, sizes and shades for scattering throughout the house and garden with an unlimited number of design possibilities. Their modular character and natural beauty make the Livingstones an ideal element for individual home design once you got accustomed to the stones' softness.

x

x

03

Swarovski "heaven is a place on earth", 2008
Address: Swarovskistraße, Wattens, Austria. **Planning partners:** Baubüro Swarovski, Norbert Berenji, Bernhard Winkler. **Client:** Daniel Swarovski & Co. **Gross floor area:** 8,000 m². **Materials:** stainless steel, white concrete, metal-mesh.

Behind the curtain

ARCHITECTS: d e signstudio
regina dahmen-ingenhoven

This sophisticated veil embraces the Swarovski factory grounds, transforming the entrance area into a landmark via a synthesis of media and acts as a gate. The semi-transparent material does not immediately reveal the factory, but allows the onlooker to deduce it instead. The opposite side of the street is incorporated in the form of a grove lined with silver limes, creating a fluid transition to the public space. Veil, landscaping, illumination and space design merge to become a breathtaking backdrop. The veil is made of a corrosion- and weather-resistant stainless steel mesh. Held in place by a ten-meter high steel stringer, it gives rise to a varied play of light and embodies a unique materiality.

01

03

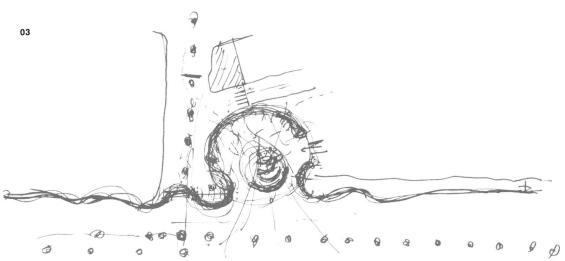

04

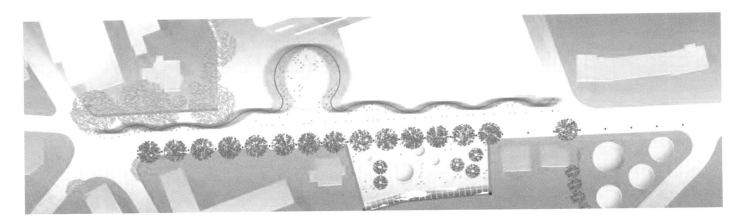

Lightfall, 2007
Address: Drusager 22, 8200 Århus, Denmark. **Project partner:** Schmidt, Hammer & Lassen Architects. **Client:** NRGI. **Gross floor area:** 50 m². **Materials:** stainless steel, optical fiber.

Let there be light

DESIGNERS: Astrid Krogh Design

Lightfall is a wall decoration inside the new NRGI office building atrium. The purpose of the 14-meter long light fixture is to underline and communicate the profile of the client. The company distributes energy as well as energy solutions and for this reason, a light feature appeared to be more appropriate than a decoration employing water. However, the designer has managed to combine both elements, resulting in a gleaming structure which appears to cascade from the upper floors. Very little energy is used to create the effect of a glowing wall thanks to optical fibers which were weaved with stainless steel treads to make the weaving stable. Lightsources produce changing colors at intervals from each other, giving the space an impression of alternating light with the possibility for a lot of different color combinations.

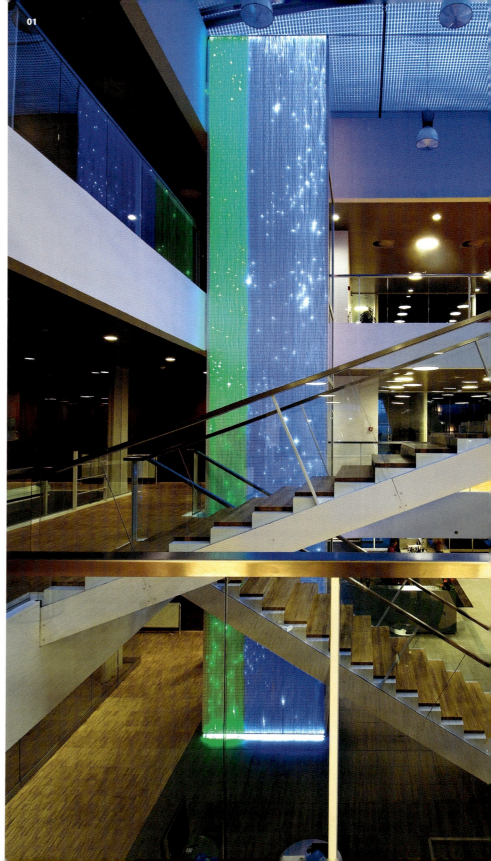

01

01 Atrium 02 Detail 03 Elevator
04 Plan of elevator with fittings for
optic fibers 05 Detail plans of fittings 06 Elevator with decoration

04

05

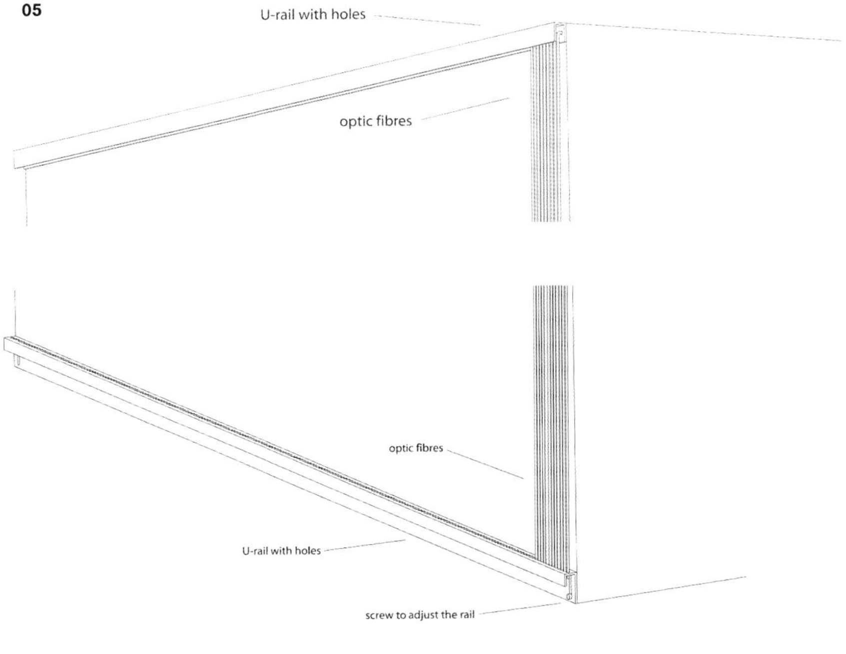

U-rail with holes

optic fibres

optic fibres

U-rail with holes

screw to adjust the rail

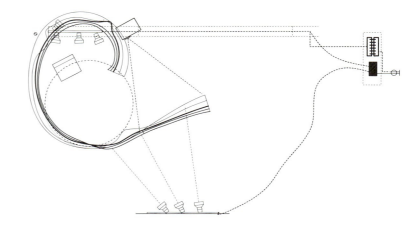

Zip Room, 2005
Address: N/A. **Planning partners:** Applied Minds,
Inc. **Client:** Herman Miller. **Materials:** flexible honey-
comb core, 3D raschel knit textiles.

Whip out your office

ARCHITECTS: Kennedy & Violich Architecture
MATx

KVA's MATx materials research unit designed the Convia
infrastructure for Herman Miller, a smart building system that allows users to change interior space configu-
rations without costly re-wiring and construction waste.
The Zip Room, an adaptable soft wall system which can
be used with Convia to create an instant enclosure, is
designed using 3-D knit fabrics of 90 percent recycled
PET polymer yarn. The Zip Room uses structural principles of tension, strength and weight reduction. The
form grammar is based on a series of digitally derived
surface geometries which can create a wide range of
curvilinear surface volumes which would be cost pro-
hibitive to realize in drywall. The fabric cladding can be
mass-customized with fit-to-measure digital fabrication
technologies.

01 Plan **02** Exterior view of the flexible wall system **03** Closeup of fabric
skin **04** View inside

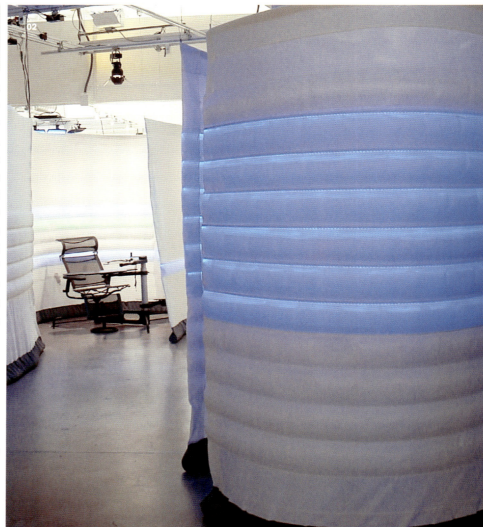

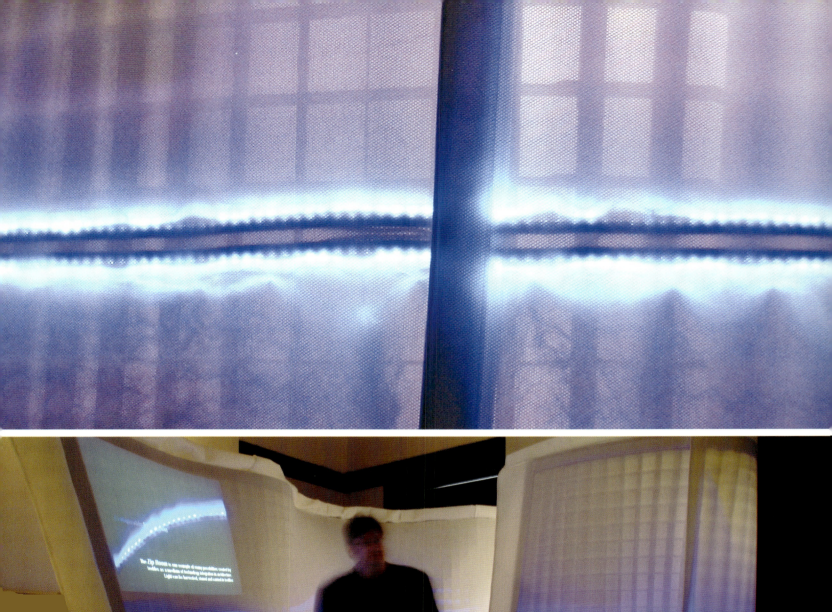

aerosystem® separator wall, 2005
Address: Theodor-Heuss-Allee 90, 60486 Frankfurt/
Main, Germany. **Planning partners:** Architekturbüro
Weller. **Client:** Sparkassen Informatik/Drehscheibe
Frankfurt/Main. **Materials:** aerosound®, acoustic effi-
cient and photometric, architectural fabric.

Wrinkle-free wall

ARCHITECTS: aeronautec
Johannes Fitz

The company's cafeteria area is optically and acoustically separated from the rest of the building using elements of the aeronautec company's aerosystem. The
flexible elements are suspended between the floor and
ceiling and together form a separating wall which can
be moved or opened at any position in order to change
the spatial layout. Individual elements consist of an
acoustically and photometrically active fabric which
allows visual spatial limitation while ensuring optimal
light penetration and diffusion. Flexible space design
and improvement of space climate were made possible
here without high costs or construction thanks to use of
modern textile fabrics.

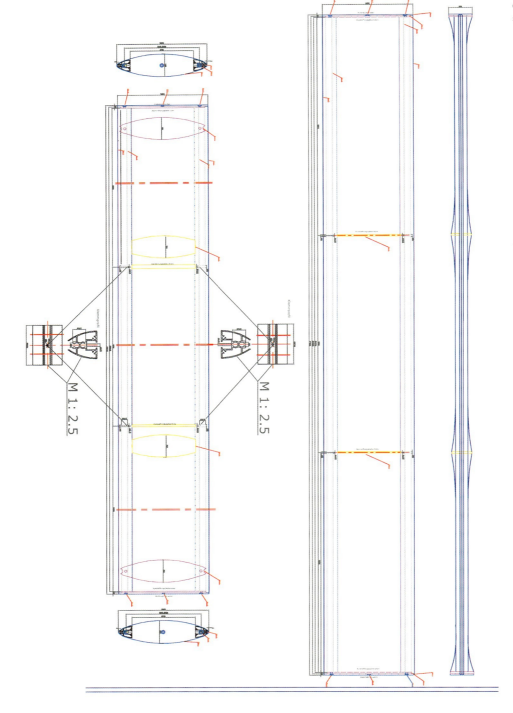

M 1 : 2.5

M 1 : 2.5

Onespace, 2006
Address: 640 West Beech Street, San Diego, CA 92101,
USA. **Planning partners:** Smith and Others with
Lloyd Russell. **Client:** David & Im Schafer. **Gross floor
area:** 39.5 m². **Materials:** stainless steel, douglas fir,
medium density fiberboard, neoprene rubber, fabric
(curtain).

Hidden treasures

ARCHITECTS: Studiomake

The designers' lives inexorably merged in the 40-
square meter space. Cooking, collecting and all other
activities take place here; therefore, a kitchen had to
be designed, storage devised, and a shop space created. Since the space is a rental, all components fulfill
terminal condition, and parts may be reused upon re-
location. The milky white curtain is suspended in front
of the floor-to-ceiling storage wall, its line and textural
qualities taken from the corrugated steel walls. It is
both a space divider and a visual silencer. When drawn
shut, it creates an ephemeral boundary between the
public living space and the more private spaces of the
home. When pulled open, it displays the artifacts of
the inhabitants' lives. This single gesture allowed the
architects to deal with light, privacy, boundaries, and
intimacy all at once.

246

01 View from terrace 02 Living space with curtain dividing the public from the more private area 03 Floor plan 04 Additional space is gained by opening the curtain 05 View of kitchen

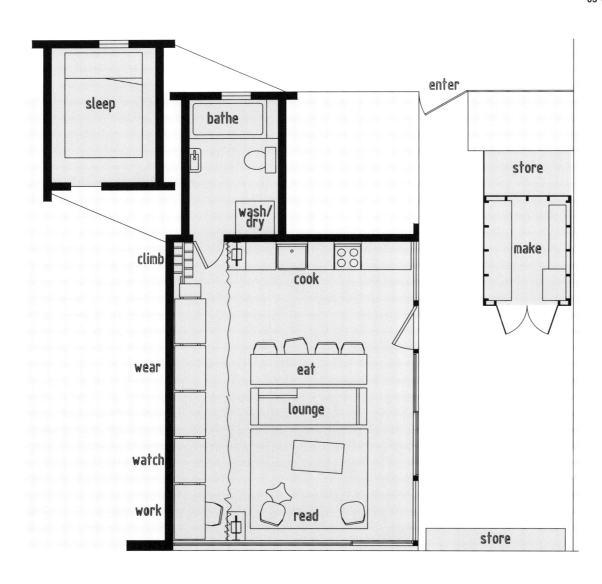

sleep

bathe

wash/dry

enter

store

make

climb

cook

wear

eat

lounge

watch

work

read

store

Index

123

360 Architecture → 64
300 West 22nd Street
Kansas City, MO 64108 (USA)
T +1.816.4723360
F +1.816.4722100
info@360architects.com
www.360architects.com

A

aeronautec GmbH → 242
Gewerbering 7
83370 Seeon (Germany)
T +49.8624.891990
F +49.8624.8919929
info@aeronautec.de
www.aeronautec.de

ag4 media facade GmbH → 20
Am Kölner Brett 8
50825 Cologne (Germany)
T +49.221.9127320
F +49.221.91273291
request@medienfassade.com
www.medienfassade.com

ASU Planungsbüro,
Dratz Construction → 32
Paul-Reusch-Straße 56
46045 Oberhausen (Germany)
T +49.208.27035
F +49.208.808269
dratz-construction@web.de
www.dratz-architekten.de

B

BEHF Ebner Hasenauer
Ferenczy ZT GmbH → 158
Kaiserstraße 41
1070 Vienna (Austria)
T +43.1.52417500
F +43.1.524175020
behf@behf.at
www.behf.at

Katrin Bethge → 202
Heiderstraße 20
20251 Hamburg (Germany)
T +49.173.6131444
info@katrinbethge.de
www.katrinbethge.de

Piet Boon Studio → 154
Ambacht 6
1511 JZ Oostzaan
(The Netherlands)
T +31.75.6559000
F +31.75.6559001
info@pietboon.nl
www.pietboon.nl

Bottega + Ehrhardt
Architekten GmbH → 114
Senefelderstraße 77A
70176 Stuttgart (Germany)
T +49.711.63303330
F +49.711.63303333
info@be-arch.com
www.be-arch.com

Ronan and Erwan Bouroullec,
SARL ERB → 122, 190
23, rue du Buisson Saint Louis
75010 Paris (France)
F +44.1.42004033
info@bouroullec.com
www.bouroullec.com

C

C18 Architekten → 100
Hölderlinstraße 40
70193 Stuttgart (Germany)
T +49.711.6566790
F +49.711.6566791
mail@c18architekten.de
www.c18architekten.de

Cadaval & Sola-Morales
Arquitectos → 176
Avenir # 1 ppal 1a
Barcelona 08006 (Spain)
T +34.93.4143714
F +34.93.4146229
studio@ca-so.com
www.ca-so.com

Camenzind Evolution Ltd. → 166
Samariterstrasse 5
8032 Zurich (Switzerland)
T +41.44.2539500
F +41.44.2539510
info@camenzindevolution.com
www.camenzindevolution.com

Curiosity, Gwenael Nicolas
→ 126
2-13-16 Tomigaya
Shibuya, Tokyo (Japan)
T +81.3.54520095
F +81.3.54549691
info@curiosity.jp
www.curiosity.jp

D

d e signstudio regina
dahmen-ingenhoven → 232
Plange Mühle 1
40221 Düsseldorf (Germany)
T +49.211.30101106
F +49.211.3010142225
drdi@ingenhovenarchitekten.eu
www.drdi.de

Despang Architekten → 50
Am Graswege 5
30169 Hanover (Germany)
T +49.511.882840
F +49.511.887985
info@despangarchitekten.de
www.despangarchitekten.de

Matteo Thun & Partners
→ 146
Via Appiani 9
20121 Milan (Italy)
T +39.02.6556911
F +39.02.6570646
info@matteothun.com
www.matteothun.com

Tjep. → 184
Veembroederhof 204
1019 HC Amsterdam
(The Netherlands)
T +31.203.624296
F +31.203.624299
goodnews@tjep.com
www.tjep.com

TONERICO:INC. → 206
902 6-18-2 Jingumae
Shibuya-ku, Tokyo 150-0001
(Japan)
T +81.3.54680608
F +81.3.54680609
tonerico.inc@nifty.com
www.tonerico-inc.com

V

**Studio Van Eijk &
Van der Lubbe** → 220
De Raadstraat 28K
5666 EA Geldrop
(The Netherlands)
T +31.40.2868636
info@ons-adres.nl
www.ons-adres.nl

Picture Credits